Eat, Drink, Animate
An Animators Cookbook

Eat, Drink, Animate
An Animators Cookbook

Tom Sito

CRC Press
Taylor & Francis Group
Boca Raton London New York

CRC Press is an imprint of the
Taylor & Francis Group, an **informa** business

CRC Press
Taylor & Francis Group
6000 Broken Sound Parkway NW, Suite 300
Boca Raton, FL 33487-2742

© 2019 by Taylor & Francis Group, LLC
CRC Press is an imprint of Taylor & Francis Group, an Informa business

No claim to original U.S. Government works

Printed on acid-free paper

International Standard Book Number-13: 978-0-8153-9976-6 (Paperback)
978-0-8153-9987-2 (Hardback)

Library of Congress Cataloging-in-Publication Data

Names: Sito, Tom, 1956- author.
Title: Eat, drink, animate : an animators cookbook / Tom Sito.
Description: Boca Raton : Taylor & Francis, a CRC title, part of the Taylor & Francis imprint, a member of the Taylor & Francis Group, the academic division of T&F Informa, plc, 2019.
Identifiers: LCCN 2018050823| ISBN 9780815399766 (paperback : acid-free paper) | ISBN 9780815399872 (hardback : acid-free paper)
Subjects: LCSH: Cooking. | Animators--Intellectual life. | Animation (Cinematography)--History. | LCGFT: Cookbooks.
Classification: LCC TX714.S5857 2019 | DDC 641.5--dc23
LC record available at https://lccn.loc.gov/2018050823

Visit the Taylor & Francis Web site at
http://www.taylorandfrancis.com

and the CRC Press Web site at
http://www.crcpress.com

To Marc & Alice Davis

Cruella de Vil, Maleficent, It's a Small World. Wonderful artists who loved cooking and entertaining. Wonderful friends, too.

Contents

List of Illustrations

Foreword

Food is an important narrative element in many an animated cartoon. Gertie the Dinosaur literally ate the scenery in her 1914 film, chomping trees as if they were celery stalks, boulders like olives, and chug-a-lugging an entire lake. Popeye's spinach helped morph a Navy wimp into a *supermensch*. Bugs Bunny eternally avoided *becoming* a meal for a Fudd-ish hunter armed with a gun and a lisp. The whale Monstro devoured an ocean's worth of tuna, as well as Pinocchio. And two dogs locking muzzles on a strand of spaghetti became an icon of first-date romance.

Veteran animator Tom Sito's delicious recipe book reveals how the creativity, imagination, and passion of animators, who have entertained moviegoers for over a century, extend to the culinary as well as the cartoon arts.

"Perhaps I could do a cookbook for animators?" muses author Sito, a Toontown light bulb appearing above his head. Indeed he could, and has done so—offering mouthwatering, toothsome sustenance *by* moving art-makers, but not just *for* them. Readers with an interest in animated movies and their makers will have those appetites, as well as their stomachs, satisfied. For much animation history is spread throughout this book, as an informative accompaniment to recipes complex and simple, from Frank & Jeanette's Special Eggs to Panama Ceviche to Szegediner Goulash, to name a few dishes in this cornucopia of yummy delights.

Some readers (and you know who you are) may not get past "Cocktails and Beverages," the opening chapter, the understandable desire for thirst-quenching delights may prove so strong. But for those who do venture forth into this animated banquet of recipes, bountiful feasts await.

To echo suave candelabra Lumiere's animated invitation, "Be our guest!"

John Canemaker

Preface

Animation is a time consuming, frustrating, and a creative job. So is cooking.

Animation requires long hours of intense concentration to detail and deep collaboration, with little guarantee of ultimate success. So does cooking.

I have been an animator for more than 40 years. I have worked on all manner of animated films, feature films, TV shows, commercials, and live action features with animated characters. I was fortunate enough to have entered the animation industry at a time when many animators of the Golden Age of Hollywood were doing their last work, and my career extended through what is now called the Second Renaissance of Animation and the Digital Revolution of the 1990s.

One thing I noticed over my years working in the studios was how many animators liked to cook. Collectively, or singularly, many artists enjoy the time preparing food and sharing it with their studio mates. It is yet another creative outlet, and many times more tangible and immediately satisfying, in contrast to our more abstract output. To us, Bart Simpson is a real living being. Yet you cannot touch him because he lives on a screen. But you can touch the grilled cheeseburgers your director just whipped up for his crew. The sharing of a communal meal has been one of the oldest ways creative teams have bonded together. Legendary writer Jules Verne recalled as a young man, he and other new writers liked to attend the dinner table of senior novelist Alexander Dumas. The old writer liked to cook for his young protégés. Verne recalled Dumas declaring, "You may criticize my style, but you dare not criticize my sauce!" Pablo Picasso went through a period where he designed and fired his own ceramic dishes. "They are good. You can eat on them," he said.

In 1976 on the animated musical *The Adventures of Raggedy Ann & Andy,* director Richard Williams gave me the opportunity to assist some scenes of the legendary animator Myron "Grim" Natwick (1890–1990). Grim began at the William Randolph Hearst Studio in the silent film era and was a major factor in the development of Betty Boop for Max Fleischer, Snow White for Walt Disney, and Nelly Bly for UPA. He taught Chuck Jones and Mark Davis how to animate. I was very young and barely out of the School of Visual Arts. I was terrified of messing up; yet somehow I got through it satisfactorily. One thing I earned as a reward was Grim's personal chili recipe, of which he was very proud.

Last year I was talking about ideas for a new book project with noted animation historian Giannalberto Bendazzi. I mentioned to him I had Grim Natwick's chili recipe, and a recipe from Walt Disney, and a studio Ghibli artist gave me Miyazaki's record on how he cooked ramen noodles for his crew when doing all-nighters. Perhaps I could do a cookbook for animators? Giannalberto immediately reacted "That is an INCREDIBLE IDEA!!" And within 48 hours I had paperwork for a publishing deal. Other top animation historians like Mindy Johnson, John

Canemaker, Charles Solomon, Dimitri Granovsky, Jim Korkis, and Jerry Beck eagerly jumped in with ideas, suggestions, and recipes of their own. Everyone wanted to join in the fun.

So here is the first attempt ever to catalog some of the favorite recipes of some of your favorite animation artists through the nearly 120 years people have been creating animated film. Among the 70 cooks listed here are ten academy award winners and five academy award nominees, including legendary animators like Chuck Jones and Frank Thomas, well-known animators from our own time like Brenda Chapman and Pete Docter, and also two bona-fide professional chefs, who had originally begun their careers in animation, then felt the urge to grow in a different direction. Other than this brief infusion of culinary professionalism, most of the recipes are home, family dishes, some complex, some fairly simple. A number of the older animators came of age during the Great Depression, and their cooking ideas reflect the rough, utilitarian simplicity of that era.

This book also illustrates the global appeal of Animation. We have recipes from animators from Italy, Japan, Iran, France, Argentina, Panama, England, Spain, Mexico, and China to name a few.

This book is not meant to analyze the psychological relationship between the artists and their personal tastes or make some profound statement about the arts as a mirror to our society. It is merely an amusing catalog, highlighting little known facts about some of our favorite cartoon creators, and as such, it is a bit of a confection in itself. I hope you enjoy reading this and trying the recipes for yourself as much as I did writing it.

Salvador Dali once cryptically declared, "It isn't art unless you can eat it." Here is a collection of recipes you can make yourself. They are good. You can eat them.

Tom Sito
October 2018

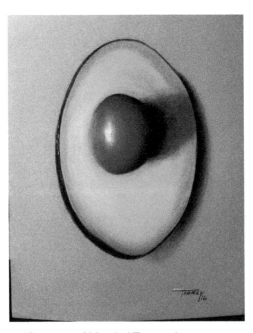

Avocado by Marshal Toomey. (Courtesy of Marshal Toomey.)

Acknowledgments

MGM Studio Club Benefit Dance, 1952. (*Tom & Jerry* copyright Turner Entertainment Co. a division or Warner Bros. Ent. Collection of the Author.)

I initially began this cookbook project much like my usual research projects. But I found as the project progressed, so many friends wanted to contribute, it really became sort of a community project or anijam. In many cases I left the contributors to describe their recipes in their own words.

Thank you to all the animation scholars who volunteered contacts and data: Charles Solomon, Nancy Beiman, John Canemaker, Jerry Beck, Jim Korkis, Didier Ghez, Giannalberto Bendazzi, Tim Callaway, Tom Minton, Marcy Carriker Smothers, the gang at the Disney Archives, Andrew Farago and the Cartoon Museum in San Francisco, and Hyperion Historical Alliance. Thank you to Onil Chibas Events, Chibasevents.com, Buzzco & Assoc., and the Chuck Jones Museum. Also the Margaret Herrick Library of the Motion Picture Academy.

Mindy Johnson did some great research on a number of the famous women in animation and wrote some of the entries about them. A great big thank you with crossed swords and gold palm to her. Thank you also to all the amazing people who volunteered their, or their family, recipes: Alice Davis, Gretchen Albrecht, Ruth Clampett, Linda Jones Clough, Rolly Crump, Hope Freleng-Shaw, Cathy Crowther, Maggie Richardson, Jennifer Grant-Castrup, Ginny and Dave Hanna, Vicky Banks, Dimitri Granovsky, Andy Luckey, Masato Suzuki, Michelle Armstrong, Holly Payne, Kevin Mack, Alan Coates, Ted Thomas, Vivien Halas, Jean Washam, and Timothy Callaway.

Thank you to the amazing Robert Lence, storyboard artist, teacher, and gourmet, for testing recipes and help with rewrites. Thank you to Rebecca Bricetti for your advice and counsel.

Thanks to Sean Connelly and Jessica Vega of Taylor & Francis, and thanks especially to my wife, Pat.

Author

Tom Sito is a veteran animator and animation historian who has worked in Hollywood for over 40 years. His screen credits include *Who Framed Roger Rabbit* (1988), *The Little Mermaid* (1989), *Beauty and the Beast* (1991), *Aladdin* (1992), *The Lion King* (1993), *Pocahontas* (1995), *The Prince of Egypt* (1998), *Shrek* (2001), and *Osmosis Jones* (2001). His television work includes *He-Man and the Masters of the Universe, She Ra Princess of Power,* and *The Superfriends.* He is President Emeritus of the Animation Guild Local 839 (Hollywood), was awarded the June Foray Award by ASIFA Hollywood, and sits on the Board of Governors for the Motion Picture Academy of Arts & Sciences. He is a member of the Hyperion Historical Alliance and The National Cartoonists Society. He currently teaches animation at the University of Southern California.

His books include *Drawing the Line: The Untold Story of the Animation Unions from Bosco to Bart Simpson* (University Press of Kentucky, 2006), *Moving Innovation: A History of Computer Animation* (MIT Press, 2013), and *Timing for Animation*, Second Edition (Focal Press, 2009).

Tom Sito by animator Jim van der Keyl.

Don Hahn and Ron Rocha cooking hot dogs for the crew, Glendale, 1989. (Collection of the Author.)

Life in an Animation Studio

Artists working on *The Yellow Submarine*, 1968. (Courtesy of the Margaret Herrick Film Archives.)

> "Any idiot who wants to create thousands of drawings for a few seconds of film is welcome to come join the club!"
>
> —Winsor McCay (1867–1934)

For more than a century, the world has delighted to the hand-drawn antics of animated characters at the movies and on TV: Mickey, Bugs, Popeye, Bart, Stewie, Buzz Lightyear, Tesuwan Atomo, Lara Croft, Mr. Rossi, to name a few. But few among the public know that the magic of these characters does not come into being in and of themselves. Bart Simpson was not just the voice actor Nancy Cartwright, or the writer James L. Brooks, or the designer Matt Groening, or the director David Silverman. Bart Simpson was all of them collectively. Mickey Mouse was not just Walt Disney. He was Walt Disney, Ub Iwerks, Freddie Moore, Noonie Davis, Wayne Alwine, Les Clark, and more. It is because animated cartoons are literally handcrafted film. Scores of artists are shaping a performance frame by frame, twenty-four frames a second. Hundreds of thousands of man (and woman) hours are committed to each project.

There are very few solitary artists in a garret in animation. Being by nature an industrialized art form, it is often a collective of hundreds of individually talented specialists, all working together to make it seem as if it was done by one hand. Despite all the good-natured hijinks you see in "making-of" videos, the reality of working in animation is you spend hundreds of hours alone, sitting at a desk, staring into a glowing screen, drawing, with concentration so intense, often you are unaware the sun had set. Animators call it "The Flow," and "Being in The Zone." Outsiders, who describe how animation is made, often describe the process as *"tedious, repetitive, exhausting work."* That is why even among other cartoonists, not everyone wants to make animation. But to those who choose animation as their living, it's really not tedious. We love doing it. We don't mind putting in the many hours required to make a character come alive. In 1938, Hollywood columnist Ted Le Berthon described animators as *"sweating artists who work at breakneck speed on monotonous routines for meager pay….the whole strange business gets in their blood. They think it, dream it, and live it."*

Rejean Bourdage animating on *Who Framed Roger Rabbit*, 1988. (Collection of the Author.)

Ken Cope working on the film *Robocop* 2, 1990. (Courtesy of Ken Cope.)

The job classifications of animation production were first defined in 1914 by cartoonist John Randolph Bray. Bray based them on the same assembly-line system that Henry Ford used to build automobiles. One artist creates designs for the characters, a writer writes the script, and a director and producer are assigned to the project and hire an art director, who oversees the design style, color models, and painted background elements. Story artists take the script, and in close collaboration with the director, create the storyboard, which becomes the blueprint of the film. In early Hollywood there were specialty story artists called gag men, whose job was to add the physical comedy (what happens when Pluto the dog has a plumber's helper stuck on his butt?, etc.). A layout artist "lays out," the staging of the particular shots with field sizes for the cameraman to refer to. The soundtrack is recorded and edited together. Meanwhile the animator creates the key poses and the beginning and end of each movement. An animation assistant "cleans up" or creates the final drawings based on the animators key frames. Other assistants add the additional "in-betweens" to flesh out an action. Additional animators who specialize in special effects add those elements, and then the final scene is checked by a quality-control artist and line-tested. When approved, the drawings are scanned, and painted, and checked again, before being shot and cut in to the work print. Production personnel oversee and track the progress of the individual scenes through the various departments.

This production process remained the industry standard until the computer revolution of the 1990s redefined the pipeline and created new job classifications for computer artists: those for modeling, lighting, rigging, and compositing; pre-visualization in the storyboard process, and motion capture artists for those specific tasks. Digital films also require software engineers and technical support, called tech directors. The tools are always being refined, and the software improved, to make important details like hair and fabric feel more real. Yet even with all the technological innovation, animation still requires many hours of intense concentration, sitting at a desk, now wielding a stylus in place of a pencil.

Anyone who has ever worked on a live action movie comes to enjoy the close proximity of the film crew during a shoot. They live like a camp of gypsies in their trailers out on location. Relationships form and even love affairs blossom. "My dear, did you hear about the star's lighting double getting it on with the 2nd Unit A.D.? When that trailer is rocking, don't bother knocking!" But that time usually lasts only about a few weeks, then a few more weeks for editing and post-production. That is nothing compared to the time needed for an animated film.

A crew on a Disney/Pixar-style film or broadcast series could expect to work in close collaboration for up to five years on a single project. One year to eighteen months for full production, the remaining three years for story work and concept development. Artists are selected as much for their willingness to collaborate as for their artistic skill. There is little time or patience to suffer a solitary mad genius. In the studio system days of Old Hollywood, crews of artists were under contract and went from film to film. A short cartoon every six weeks. Frank Thomas and Ollie Johnston, the famous master animators, went from graduating Stanford University right into the Walt Disney Studio and spent 46 years creating superb animation on film after film. Artist Floyd Gottfredson worked 45 years just drawing one thing, the Mickey Mouse comic strip. On Disney's *101 Dalmatians*, one animator spent an entire year just animating the spots on the dogs. The team that created *The Simpsons* show has been working on those characters season after season for thirty years. The old saying in the business is you work with the same people, only the producers and companies change. The small cadre of people who create animation mostly all know each other. They can expect to work with each other at several different studios.

In 1988, at the world premiere of *Who Framed Roger Rabbit*, live-action director Robert Zemeckis said about his experience working with animators, *"I don't know how you guys do it. I'm used to getting together my team, taking some cameras and some lights, and going out and shooting a few setups. You guys come together and you live like a family! You marry each other, have each other's children, and bury each other's grandfathers. Then the film ends and phffffit! You all scatter...."*

Warner Bros. artists on a *skiing weekend*, 1939. (Courtesy of Martha Goldman-Sigal.)

Such collaboration at such close quarters creates an esprit de corps rare in the art world. The camaraderie of such a team effort encouraged team activities, like bowling leagues, baseball games, golf tournaments, paintball games, country dances, and such. It is common for animation artists to marry within the profession. For instance, I am an animator with 32 feature films to my credit, while my wife Pat is a painter-checker with 53 films to her credit. Both Walt Disney and his brother Roy married Ink & Paint girls. Animator Lee Blair, the brother of animator Preston Blair, married Mary Blair, the famous animation color designer. Animation storyboard artist and director Brenda Chapman (*The Lion King, Brave*) met at work and married storyboard artist and director Kevin Lima (*Tarzan, Enchanted*). And so it goes.

Outside of Walt Disney, most animation units were not the primary focus of a movie company, yet animation required significant office space to accommodate large numbers of artists. So producers usually looked for cheap industrial space: old warehouses, cheap furniture. Dave Deitich's LA studio in the 1930s was a converted pickle factory. Every room had floors that inclined to a center drain. Your pencils would regularly roll off your desk. In the Leon Schlesinger studio, the *Looney Tunes* and *Merrie Melodies* cartoons were created in a dilapidated building on Van Ness Avenue known as Termite Terrace, today adjacent to the entrance of television station KTLA. It was considered such a dump, when you finished a Coke, instead of tossing it in the wastepaper basket, you punched a hole in the wall and tossed it in. For a time, the Canadian studio Nelvana was in a converted waterfront warehouse. During the winter, large hempen ropes were draped around the building to prevent people from being blown into icy Lake Ontario. The animation crews, made to spend 46–70 hours a week there, did their best to make these spaces cozy.

Bugs Bunny animator Ben Washam, who had once been a short-order cook during the Great Depression, would whip up dishes for his fellow artists during breaks. Gag man Cal Howard actually kept a hot-dog steamer at his desk to serve friends an impromptu snack. At Walt Disney's Hyperion Studio, receptionist Mary Flannigan had a busy side business selling the staff cigarettes, chewing gum, aspirin, candy, and hard-boiled eggs. Disney layout man Bill Herwig kept a cast-iron hibachi stove under his desk, and after work would cook oriental dishes he learned working on cargo freighters across the South Pacific. At Hanna-Barbera, director Bill Hanna liked to occasionally cook a southwestern American barbeque for his far-flung overseas outlets, like his crews in Spain and Australia. During the heaviest part of overtime, Japanese artists at the Ghibli Studio would take turns cooking for the crew. Even director Hayao Miyazaki would take his turn and personally cook for his team.

Studios that could afford it created an eating space for their team. Besides keeping people's energy levels up, keeping meals in studio actually saved the time that would otherwise be spent driving or walking to or from an outside eatery. When DreamWorks was set up in 1995, a big thing was made about their cafeteria serving free lunches. I once timed myself going out to get lunch and bring it back to my desk. Because we were in an industrial park in Glendale, the fastest one could drive out, grab a lunch, park, and return was 45 minutes. The average was more like an hour and a half. By providing lunch, most DreamWorks animators ate in about 20 minutes and returned to work. The studio earned the benefit of that increased productivity. Walt Disney famously had a commissary at his state-of-the-art studio lot in Burbank, and also a private penthouse club. The Ink & Paint Department had its own tearoom for afternoon breaks. Many artists, to save money, still brown-bagged it or patronized the catering trucks parked outside the main gate. When the animators of MGM on *Tom and Jerry* were working late, the main studio granted them permission to use the studio cafeteria. Management assumed they would be using the hamburger stand. Instead, the animators thought they meant the main cafeteria where Clark Gable and Judy Garland ate. They rushed in and filled up on free steaks, lamb chops, and "crème brûlée." After studio operations got the first bills, they quickly realized their mistake and banished the animators to the more modest hamburger stand.

MGM short film directors at the MGM cafeteria, circa 1937. L-R, Rudy Ising, Hugh Harman, Paul Smith, Producer Fred Quimby, unknown. (Courtesy of the Margaret Herrick Film Archives.)

The transition of animation from pencil and paint to digital has changed jobs' titles, but not the communal spirit of a creative bullpen. As long as creative people come together in a bullpen to make a film, regardless of technology, the urge towards a community spirit generated by the sharing of a common meal will continue.

Cocktails and Beverages

Tom Sito, in Manhattan, with a Manhattan.

66 For you there will always be a candle in the refrigerator, and a martini left burning in the window. 99

—Mary Blair

Since the beginning of the medium, animators have liked a nice drink after work.

Or at lunch.

Or even during work!

Great animation demands intense amounts of focus and concentration. Creative egos would clash passionately over their ideas to improve a scene or make a gag funnier. Over the years I've seen people punch the walls and throw stacks of paper out a window in frustration. Story man Bill Peet once got so angry at Walt Disney during a disagreement over the opening scene of *Bambi*, that he threw a bottle of Higgins India ink at his head (he missed). So after such pressure, as a mental release from that intense focus, many animators were known to "loosen the strings" as it were, when the time came. Jack Kinney, who directed the *Sport Goofy* cartoon shorts, put it this way: "We worked together. We played together. We drank together," he said. "Maybe more ideas were quenched than born in our frequent forays to favorite bars for liquid inspiration."

London Animators on a Pub Night circa 1988. (Collection of the Author.)

The animation studio had evolved out of the newspaper business of the turn of the century. Many first generation animators initially wanted to be newspaper cartoonists and went into the flicker business as a fall-back career. As anyone who ever saw the play *The Front Page* or read H. L. Mencken knows, the pressroom was known for its hard-drinking, cigar-chomping, tobacco-spitting atmosphere. Some cartoonist-writers like James Thurber (*The Unicorn in the Garden*) and Walt Kelly (*Pogo*) were well known tipplers. Chuck Jones animator Ben Washam told me Walt Kelly could get so drunk that if he tried to stand up, he would topple over, yet in that inebriated state, he would sit and hand-ink his comic strip, including the lettering. Anyone who has ever done that type of line work with crow quill pen, or brush, knows even the slightest tremble in your hand will show in the line work. But Ben said Walt Kelly's hand was solid as a rock. All his focus was in keeping his drawing hand steady.

When legendary animator Art Babbitt passed away in 1992, historian Jerry Beck and I organized his memorial service at Hollywood Presbyterian Church. While sifting through old photos and sketches, his wife Barbara appeared in the door holding a large bottle of Glenfiddich. "This is Art's scotch," she said with solemnity. "Art hated anyone he didn't know getting into his scotch. But I think he would want you to have a drink now. So Tom, would you like a scotch?" I said I would be honored. Barbara then turned to Jerry and said "Jerry, would you like a scotch?" Jerry shyly confessed, "I would, err, but I really don't drink." Barbara then said "Oh. I see. I'll get you a beer, then."

When I began in animation in the mid 1970s, it was the tail end of the "Mad-Men Era" in American advertising. Many of the animation houses that worked with ad agency people made no attempt to conceal their liquor cabinet. Part of making a client welcome could be to pour them a drink. I noticed all the senior animators over me were Scotch drinkers. They wouldn't trust you if you asked for just a Coke, or a wine-spritzer. At Filmation Studios (*Fat Albert, HeMan, SheRa*), every Friday at afternoon break, a cocktail party would break out studio wide.

There were a number of well-known watering holes for studio animators. In New York during the 1930s, many cartoonists, including those who worked for *The New Yorker*, preferred a former speakeasy called Costello's Bar on East 44th Street. (Today it is called the Overlook.) Many cartoonist drawings still adorn its walls. During the 1930s Hyperion phase of Walt Disney Studios, many young artists would get a "two-bit beer" at Charlie Rivers. He was a local bootlegger who dispensed his home brew and even counseled artists on their careers in animation. Later after Prohibition's repeal, so many liked going to a roadhouse called The Tam O' Shanter that they nicknamed it "The Commissary." When Walt Disney Studio moved to their Burbank lot, the preferred gin mills became Alphonses, the Pago-Pago Lounge, and the Smoke House. For a time, Alphonses, or "Alphos," was so popular that Walt Disney issued a memo to his animators forbidding them to go there anymore (for once they ignored him). Hanna and Barbera liked the Smoke House so much they had a designated table, just behind the headwaiter's station.

Walt Disney could be seen among the Hollywood glitterati at well-known Tinseltown hangouts like Chasens, the Brown Derby, the Cocoanut Grove, Musso & Franks, and Ciros. Supposedly, it was a chance meeting in 1935 over dinner at Chasens with classical conductor Leopold Stokowski that got Walt thinking about an animated classical concert, which became *Fantasia*.

In the 1960s when much animation work had transitioned from theatrical shorts to TV shows and commercial work, Boardners Bar in Hollywood and Charles & Company in Studio City were hangouts. Filmation artists out in the San Fernando Valley went to The Bunker. I once went to a barbeque place near DePatie Freleng called the Valley Ranch for lunch. When I ordered a draft beer with a shot of Jack Daniels on the side, the waitress said, "Say, you're an animator, aren't you?" For Pixar animators, The Hidden City Café was the hangout while working on *Toy Story*. For a long time, the working title of *Monsters Inc.* was "Hidden City." They also built a hidden Tiki Bar within the maze of their artist's cubicles. During the glory period of London commercial animation in Soho, the Friday night Pub Night was a holy obligation. Animators at Richard Williams, Halas & Batchelor, Klacto, Mike Smith, Hibbert/ Ralph and others would phone each other and coordinate a single pub. That evening the entire animation community would meet over a pint. It was hard to remain angry with your supervisor when he was the one buying the next round. The Star & Garter on Poland Street, and the Green Man on Wardour Street were popular hangouts. When the Don Bluth Studio was in Dublin working on *An American Tail* and *The Land Before Time*, the artist's favorite place to grab a pint of Guinness was The DeerPark Inn. The animators of Toronto animation studio Nelvana liked an adjacent bar and fish restaurant called The Skipper.

Disney Animators Partying at the Hotel Norconian in 1938. (Courtesy of The Animation Guild, Local # 839 Archives.)

During the financially lean 1930s–1940s, many studio artists after work would save money on restaurants by throwing house parties. Strictly a bring-your-own-bottle, potluck affair. They would spin records on a record player, dance, and drink whatever was made or brought in. In the 1990s, Disney animator Dave Spafford missed the British custom of pub night on Fridays that he got to experience when working in London on *Who Framed Roger Rabbit*. He and his wife Debbie decided to turn their entire North Hollywood home into a pub. Everyone brought their favorite beverages and snacks. Dave even created a game room with a pool table and pinball machines. Famous animators like Ralph Bakshi, Glen Keane, Richard Williams, Don Bluth, and even English rock-and-roll singer Rick Astley dropped in. The Spaff Night was a weekly tradition for about ten years. It only ended when all of Dave's neighbors en masse threatened to kill him and burn his house down.

Here are some mixed drink recipes from that tradition.

RECIPES

Marc Davis

Marc Davis (1913–2000) was a top Disney animator, designer, teacher, and author. His talents gave life to Maleficent, Cruella da Vil, and *The Pirates of the Caribbean*. Marc and his artist-wife Alice loved entertaining and good food, and Marc loved his martini. Disney legend Grim Natwick told animation historian John Canemaker, *"His [Marc's] gin martini has long been recognized as the finest martini west of the Mississippi. Never to have tasted a Marc Davis martini is to have been denied an experience unparalleled in drinking tradition."*

The Marc Davis Martini

Ingredients

* ❋ 2 ounces of unchilled Gilbey's Gin or vodka
* ❋ One bottle cap of extra-dry vermouth
* ❋ Stuffed green olive or twist of lemon rind

Directions

Pour vodka over ice—one or two cubes depending on preference. Pour a very small amount of the extra-dry vermouth into the bottle cap (never pour vermouth from bottle directly into glass). Splash several drops of vermouth into the glass and return remaining vermouth in cap to bottle. Stir with slow, broad circular strokes just a few times. Never stir by swishing glass. Add a twist of lemon rind, peeling carefully to avoid getting any of the white (bitter) pith.

The Tinker Bell Cocktail was created in 1990 to celebrate the restoration of the 100-year-old Imperial Hotel in Tokyo. It was a favorite of Marc Davis.

Tinker Bell Cocktail

Ingredients

* 1.2 ounces white rum
* 0.3 ounce peach liqueur
* 0.3 ounce parfait amour or violet liqueur
* 0.02 ounce (1 teaspoon) lemon juice

Directions

Garnish with a green mint cherry in bottom of glass and rim the glass with sugar.

Mary Blair

Mary Blair (1911–1978) was one of the top animation designers at the Walt Disney Studio. Her work influenced *Saludos Amigos, Three Caballeros*, and *Peter Pan*.

Mary Blair Martini

Mary's niece Denise Chamberlain recalled they drank classic 3:1 martinis (Martini & Rossi vermouth). Gilbey's gin was in a clear glass bottle, mixed in an elegant tall, narrow glass pitcher filled with ice and stirred with a glass teardrop rod. I remember olives, but maybe onions were there too. Even though they were in a pitcher of ice, they didn't sit around long enough to become diluted.

Denise also recalled in the 1960s Mary shifted from gin to vodka martinis, made much like Marc Davis' martini. The Blairs and Davises liked to party together.

Mary Blair's martini set. (Courtesy of Maggie Richardson.)

James Bodrero

James Bodrero (1900–1980) was a concept artist and screenwriter for Walt Disney. His work can be seen in *Fantasia, Dumbo,* and *The Three Caballeros.*

The Bodrero Special, Invented at Mary and Lee Blair's Home

Re-animated by John Canemaker.

"*The* drink" for the Disney studio crowd in the 1940s and 50s "was martinis straight up," Roland "Rolly" Crump, Disney Imagineer, told John Canemaker in 1995. "That's what everybody drank."

It was in Lee and Mary Blair's kitchen, at a party one evening in 1939, that the "James Bodrero Punch" or "The Special" was born. It was recalled by Mary's good friends, Marc and Alice Davis, to John Canemaker in a 1994 interview.

Ingredients

* 1 bottle of gin
* 1 bottle of chablis
* 1 bottle of soda
* 1 cake of ice containing assorted fruits
* 1 sliced cucumber

Directions

Pour all liquids over the cake of ice containing the fruit. Add cucumber slices to "smooth" it.

"The drink was so smooth and tastes so good," said Alice Davis, Disney costume designer, in 1994, "you don't realize what you're drinking until they pick you up off the floor."

WARNING

James Bodrero almost electrocuted himself the night he invented his drink at the Blairs': he used an electric iron to make space in a block of ice for the punch's fruit!

And so, as Mr. Elmer Fudd often said, "Be vewy, vewy careful."

Chris Bailey

Chris Bailey is from Portland Oregon and was a Disney animator on films like *The Little Mermaid, Runaway Brain, the Lion King*, and *Tarzan*. He became a successful animation director on live-action hybrid projects like *Garfield the Movie* and *Alvin and the Chipmunks*.

Classic Grog

It's kind of like a rum old fashioned.

In the 1700s, Royal Navy Admiral Verson, nicknamed "Old Grog" for his coat (a coarse textured fabric), was the first to cut his sailor's daily tot (rum ration) with water. He knew that a boatload of drunken sailors probably wasn't the best way to run a ship, so he divided the daily rum ration (1/2 pint) into two servings and mixed with water for a water-to-rum ratio of 4:1. He offered sugar, limes, and nutmeg for purchase to make it more palatable.

Ingredients

- ❋ My grog of choice is 1/4 ounce fresh lime juice (no exceptions)
- ❋ 1/2 ounce rock candy syrup (demerara sugar dissolved in water 2:1)
- ❋ 2 1/4 ounces Caidenhead navy rum
- ❋ Dust with a few shakes of ground nutmeg
- ❋ Stir and add ice

I prefer a big square cube, but that's mostly because they're more convenient to make than ice balls and won't dilute the booze too quickly.

Pete Docter

Pete Docter was born in Minnesota. He became one of Pixar's top animation directors and story artists, writing and directing classics like *Monsters Inc., Up*, and *Inside Out*. In 2018 he became the creative head of Pixar.

Basil Gimlet

Ingredients

* 2 ounces gin (I prefer Hendricks or 209)
* Juice of 1/2 fresh lime
* 1/2 ounce simple syrup
* 5 basil leaves

Directions

Start by muddling basil leaves in a pint glass. Add other ingredients plus ice; shake for 30 seconds. Serve in martini glass with sugar rim.

Walt Disney

Walt Disney (1901–1966) "If you had a working meeting in Walt's private office, most times he would serve you a glass of V-8 vegetable juice. However, 5 o'clock was drink time in the office," recalled one of Walt Disney's last secretaries, Tommie Wilck. "If you were in the office at 5 o'clock, we always served drinks. Walt had a Scotch Mist and I always served whatever anybody else wanted."

Scotch Mist

Serves 1

Ingredients

* Crushed ice
* 2–3 ounces of Scotch (Walt liked Canadian Club or Black & White)
* Twist of lemon peel or orange slice
* Long silver or plastic spoon (optional)

Directions

Pack crushed ice into a glass. Pour Scotch over ice. Stir. Garnish with lemon or orange.

Nancy Beiman

Nancy Beiman is an animator from New Jersey. Her credits include Walt Disney's *Treasure Planet, Hercules, Fantasia 2000* and the *Goofy Movie.*

Beiman Family Recipe for Brooklyn Egg Creams

Ingredients

* U-Bet chocolate syrup (*Dad said "nothing else will do" and he was right*); I use dark chocolate
* Milk (cow's or chickpea, it has to foam)
* Seltzer (*never use club soda or tonic water!*)

Tools:

* 12-ounce heavy soda glass
* Long-handled steel spoon
* Seltzer maker if you have one, bottle of seltzer if you have not (do NOT use club soda!)
* Straw (paper or steel)

Directions

* Chill the glass in the fridge for a while. Then take it out and add 2 "shpritzes" (about one tablespoon) of U-Bet to the glass. Add some milk on top. Not too much, this is not a milkshake! The proportion, although it can vary, should be 2 parts U-bet to 1 part milk. Equal parts are fine and make a thicker "head" on the drink.
* Now fill the glass up with seltzer. The milk will give it a "head." Then take the long spoon and stir the drink by "pulling" the syrup from the bottom of the glass to the top. It should not be stirred the way you stir an ordinary drink.
* Drink this with a straw. No one drinks it from the glass. It's also usually drunk quickly since the "bite" from the seltzer, and the "head" from the milk, are temporary. It's why you cannot buy bottled egg creams.

Enjoy!

Raul Garcia-Sanz

Raul Garcia-Sanz was born in Madrid, Spain. Raul has animated all around the world. He is chiefly known for his work on Don Bluth's *Land Before Time, Lucky Luke,* Walt Disney's *Who Framed Roger Rabbit, Aladdin, Hercules,* and his own film *Extraordinary Tales.*

Spanish Sangria Raul Garcia Style

Ingredients

* 1 bottle of red wine
* 4 cans of 7-Up, Sprite, or similar soda
* 1/2 wine glass of any spirited liquor like rum, Cognac, Grand Marnier, vodka, Pacharán (sloe gin)
* 2 peaches
* 1 pear
* 6 oranges
* 2 lemons
* 4 spoonful of sugar
* 1 cinnamon stick
* Lots of ice

Directions

The day before: Chop and dice all the peaches and pears, two of the oranges, and one lemon in slices or cubes (peel the peaches and pears, leave the oranges and lemons with their peel), and soak them in an bowl with the juice of two oranges and the other lemon, the spoons of sugar and the cinnamon stick, adding a dash of the spirits. Rum, triple sec, Grand Marnier, and Cointreau work the best. The fruitier it is, the better. Vodka and Cognac also work really good. My personal touch: A dash of Pacharan, a sloe gin prepared in the Basque Country, hard to find outside Spain. It gives a light, sweet anisette fruity touch. The more time you leave the fruit soak in the mix, the more the fruit will absorb the alcohol, key for a great Sangria. My personal recipe includes the "whatever hard liquors are around the house" or the famous "whatever was inside the minibar I raided on my last trip." Store the mix in the freezer till next day.

Next day: Fill a big punch bowl with ice. Pour the whole bottle of red wine. The younger and fruitier is the wine, the best the Sangria will taste. Beaujolais Nouveau is pretty good. Rioja tempranillo, of course, or in California, Pinot Noir or Chardonnay will do the trick. Don't expend much money in a really good wine. The key is in the mix of alcohol-soaked fruits. Add the soda. For a bottle of wine, add 3–4 cans. It is up to you to add more wine or soda to change the strength. Mix with the frozen liquored fruit bowl from the freezer and add the juice of a couple extra fresh oranges. Stir well, mix everything, and serve it very cold.

One extra trick: You can buy cheap white wine in tetra brick or a carton container and let it freeze for a couple of days prior. Substitute part of the ice for the block of frozen white wine (once "peeled" from the carton container). That way the Sangria will keep its kick for a little bit longer.

Drink with moderation. The best sangrias drink easy like water and kick like a mule but you shouldn't have a next-day hangover.

Jon Schnepp

Jon Schnepp (1967–2018) was an animator, director, and voice artist. He worked on *Space Ghost Coast to Coast, Aqua Teen Hunger Force,* and *Metalocalypse* and directed videos for numerous heavy metal bands. His favorite drink was a Pickelback.

Picklebacks

Ingredients

* One jigger of George Dickel Tennessee whiskey (or your preferred whiskey)
* One jigger of sour dill pickle juice

Directions

- Throw back one, then the other.
- Repeat.

Chris Prynoski

Chris Prynoski is an animator, director, and producer. He founded the studio Titmouse. He is known for TV programs such as Metalocalypse, Freaknik: The Musical, Motorcity and Megas XLR, and he contributed to films such as *Beavis and Butt-Head Do America*.

The Hillbilly X-Treme!

Ingredients

* 2 ounces cheap well whiskey
* 8 ounces Mountain Dew in a CAN (extra good if you get the old-school recipe with sugar instead of corn syrup)
* 1 squirt fake lime juice (like the kind that comes in a plastic lime; you could use a real lime, but that would make it classier)
* A few ice cubes
* Some duct tape

Directions

Open the can of Mountain Dew and pour the contents into a cup or some other container. Saw off the top of the Mountain Dew can or cut it off with scissors. Throw away the top of the can (or recycle it if you can!) Use the duct tape to cover the sharp edge of the can. Go all the way around. You don't want to get a bleeding lip! Throw a few ice cubes into the can. Pour in the cheap whiskey. Fill up the rest of the can with the Mountain Dew you poured out earlier, add a liberal squirt of lime juice, and give it a quick swirl with your middle finger. Lick off your finger and point it at your favorite authority figure as you slowly sip your drink, staring them directly in the eyes.

You have now enjoyed a Hillbilly X-Treme!

Fun fact: Mountain Dew was originally invented as a mixer for whiskey.

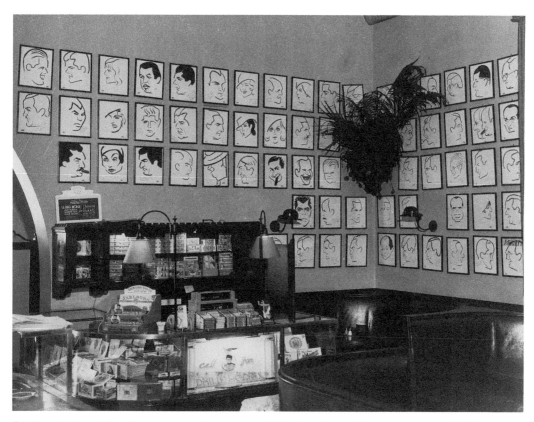

Cashier station at The Brown Derby Restaurant, 1936. (Courtesy of the Margaret Herrick Film Archives.)

Breakfast and Brunch

Walter Lantz presenting the Woody Woodpecker mural at a military hospital, 1945. (Collection of the Author.)

Nancy Beiman

The first female graduate of the Cal Arts character animation program was New Jersey native **Nancy Beiman**. Her credits include Walt Disney's *Treasure Planet, A Goofy Movie, Fantasia 2000*, and *Hercules*. She is also the author of several popular books on creating animation and has taught and lectured around the world.

The Beiman family (Jack and Sally and their children Melvyn, Elliott, and Ceil) ran small restaurants and lunch counters from the Great Depression well into the fifties. Here are some of their recipes.

Sesame Beagle, Drawing by Nancy Beiman. (Courtesy of Nancy Beiman.)

Challah French Toast

Ingredients

- Allow 2 pieces of challah (egg) bread per person. Get it fresh if you can. (No, it doesn't have to be stale.) Cut the slices medium thick but not too thick.
- 4 or 5 medium eggs (*for a vegan version, mix 1 tbsp ground flaxseed or chia to 3 tbsp water for each 'egg' and add 2 tsp nutritional yeast to the mixture, beat well with a fork, and let stand 5 minutes*)
- Dash of milk (*I use chickpea or hemp milk, you may use coconut or cow milk*)
- Sprinkling of nutmeg and cinnamon
- Coconut oil (or butter). Coconut oil is best; it does not burn.

Directions

- Beat the eggs with a fork in a large shallow bowl. (*Dad broke the eggs one-handed; I'd show you how, but it can't be described verbally.*) Mix in some cinnamon and nutmeg. Add a dash of whatever kind of milk you are using.
- Soak the bread in the egg or flaxseed mixture while heating the coconut oil in a cast-iron skillet or other kind of wide skillet. Turn the bread to soak both sides.
- Once the oil has melted, put one or two slices of the bread in the skillet and fry them at medium temperature until nicely browned on one side. Flip with a spatula and brown the other side.
- Serve with a small drizzle of maple syrup and a side of some lettuce and fruit.

The Secret of Perfect Poached Eggs

Forget the "egg poachers" and simply add a dash of salt and three tablespoons of white vinegar to 2 inches of water boiling in your cast-iron skillet. Carefully break the eggs, one at a time, into a saucer. (Best done one-handed.) Stir the water in one direction with a spoon; then slide each egg into the boiling water; the vinegar will cause the whites to "set" immediately. Simmer uncovered for 3 to 5 minutes. Remove with a slotted spoon and serve over toasted buttered bread.

Joe Grant

Joe Grant (1908–2005) was a Walt Disney story artist and designer. He worked for Walt Disney from *Three Little Pigs* (1934) until *Cinderella* (1949). Teamed with Dick Huemer, he influenced a lot of *Dumbo*, and his cocker spaniel was the inspiration for Lady in the film *Lady and the Tramp*.

Joe left Disney in 1949 to run his own ceramics and greeting card company. In 1992 when his wife Jenny was dying, she said to him, "Joe, after I'm gone, you'll go nuts here by yourself. Why don't you go back to work?" So he accepted the studios offer to return for the Disney Renaissance. He contributed to modern classics like *Aladdin, The Lion King, Pocahontas*, and *Monsters Inc.* Pixar's *Up* is dedicated to him. Into his 90s he possessed an amazing constitution, and still had a memory sharp as a tack. He gave the studio a living link to its famous past. He provided the type of gentle, yet charming classic Disney humor that seemed untainted by the cynicism of the later generations. He used to say to me, "The difference between us is you work for Disney's, while I work for WALT Disney."

Oatmeal

This is from his daughter Jennifer:

"First Eat Your Oatmeal." JG

Joe Grant loved his sand dabs and French pastries. All fine to enjoy as long as the day started with *OATMEAL*. He learned about the health benefits of eating oatmeal and chewing his food slowly from his grandfather who had lived a long, productive life and also enjoyed French pastries.

Here's Joe's oatmeal recipe as vividly remembered by his granddaughter Diane who ate more than her share: Marina is the name of Joe's dog.

- In a 32-ounce Pyrex measuring cup, combine 1/2 cup of McCann's quick-cooking imported Irish Oats with 1 cup of water. Add a pinch of salt and stir well.
- Place uncovered mixture in microwave while being careful to avoid tripping over Marina under foot.
- Microwave on high for 2 minutes. When you hear the ding, remove oatmeal, and allow it to stand for 1 minute before serving.
- Add sugar and half and half to taste.
- While chewing each bite of your nutritious oatmeal 20 times, leisurely peruse the latest *New Yorker* or *LA Times* Comics section.
- Fill Marina's bowl with the remaining oatmeal, adding a dollop of cottage cheese and one leftover sand dab.

Christmas Witch by Joe Grant. (Collection of the Author.)

Just shy of his 97th birthday, Joe Grant passed away gently, at home at his drawing table. He was working on one more drawing, which he completed.

Chuck Jones

Chuck Jones. (Courtesy of The Chuck Jones Museum.)

Charles M. Jones, better known as **Chuck Jones (1912–2002)** was one of the great Hollywood animation directors, many of his short cartoons of Bugs Bunny, Daffy Duck, Pepe LePew, and the Roadrunner & Wiley Coyote are considered classics today. After leaving Warner Bros., he created classic TV specials like *The Grinch Who Stole Christmas* (1964). Chuck was a raconteur and ambassador for animation around the world. He championed the notion that animation should be respected as a serious art form.

This is from his daughter, Linda Jones-Clough. (The Dorothy she mentions was Chuck's first wife and her mom.)

Eggs Goldenrod and Orange Juices Brunch

"Eggs Goldenrod" and *"Orange Juices"* Brunch (about six servings, not six people! Many people like more than one serving…so be forewarned)

Ingredients	
❋ 1 quart orange juice (fresh squeezed)	❋ 2 pounds bacon
❋ 6 maraschino cherries	❋ 6 slices sour dough bread (very sour)
❋ 1½ teaspoons Angostura bitters (optional), divided	❋ Butter for toast (optional)
	❋ 8 tablespoons butter (real butter!)
❋ 1 bottle Champagne, sparkling cider, other sparkling wine	❋ 8 tablespoons flour (white flour)
	❋ 2 teaspoons salt
❋ 6 sprigs of mint	❋ 4 cups evaporated milk
❋ 8 eggs	❋ Paprika

For the "Orange Juices"

(If you are serving these before breakfast, you will certainly need to double or triple this recipe…)

Fill 8-ounce glass 1/2 full with orange juice. Add 1/4 teaspoon Angostura bitters (optional… not to everyone's taste), 1 maraschino cherry, fill glass with sparkling beverage, garnish with mint. Cheers! Chuck and Dorothy (and their guests) usually drank at least one, sometimes two, before she started to prepare breakfast…then another with prep and, probably, another at the table…

Eggs

Hard boil the **eggs**. *(Egg preparation can be done the night before. It doesn't matter if they are cold.)* Cool. Separate yolks from the whites and set aside in a bowl. Cut or tear egg whites into bite-sized pieces and set aside in a bowl. Coarsely grate egg yolks and set aside. *(If you are doing this the night before, cover each bowl and refrigerate.)*

Bacon

2 pounds bacon, cooked crispy… Chuck always said there is "never enough bacon," so, if two pounds is not going to be enough to make sure everyone has "more than enough," make it 3 or 4 pounds. Keep warm in a very low oven (temperature, not elevation).

Toast

Toast all slices of sourdough bread to golden brown (or, as Dorothy often did, scrape off the burned parts in the sink and don't tell anyone). Wrap in aluminum foil and put in oven with the bacon. You can butter the toast if you want to…sometimes she did and sometimes she didn't. If you want more toast, go ahead and make some more…and butter it.

Plates

If you like warm plates, you could put the plates in the oven to warm, too.

White Sauce

This was Chuck's favorite sauce…he loved creamed peas, creamed carrots, creamed carrots and peas, creamed tuna, creamed chicken… but most of all, Eggs Goldenrod. Here is the way Dorothy prepared the sauce:

- In a medium-size saucepan, heat **milk** over med-low heat (scald, do not boil…you can heat in a microwave, but don't boil milk!)
- In another medium-size saucepan, melt **butter** over moderately low heat. Remove from heat and slowly whisk in flour and salt. Return to heat and cook 3 minutes, without browning, stirring constantly (and I mean constantly!). Remove from heat and gradually add hot milk, whisking constantly, until all the milk has been added and sauce is smooth. Return to heat and cook for about 5 minutes, stirring constantly, until mixture is smooth and thickened.
- Remove from heat and add **egg whites**. Return to heat and stir egg whites into sauce for 1 minute or so, just long enough to heat the eggs.

To Assemble and Serve

Take bacon and toast out of oven. Heap bacon on a large platter and put on the dining table or serving counter for people to help themselves.

Put a slice of toast on each (warm) plate. Ladle creamed eggs over toast. Sprinkle about 2 tablespoons of grated egg yolk over the middle of the creamed eggs and add a pinch (or dash or 1/4 teaspoon) of paprika to the center of the grated egg yolks.

Grab your fourth "orange juice" and enjoy. (Warning, this dish cools quickly and is not nearly as good when it's cold.)

Note: Chuck and Dorothy didn't bother with coffee with this meal, but sometimes added a bowl of fresh fruit or coffee cake on the side.

Frank Thomas

Frank Thomas (1912–2004) was one of the great animators of Walt Disney's Nine Old Men. While modestly insisting Marc Davis and Milt Kahl were the better artists than him, Frank animated some of the most memorable moments in Disney history: Bambi and Thumper on the ice, Pinocchio singing "I Got No Strings," Captain Hook, Baloo singing "Look for the Bare Necessities," Winnie the Pooh, and the Queen of Hearts. With his livelong friend and colleague Ollie Johnston, he authored the seminal book, Disney Animation: the Illusion of Life. He was also the piano player in the band The Firehouse Five.

Here is Frank's son Ted Thomas and his wife Kuniko Okubo remembering a favorite recipe of his parents:

1946 was a big year for my parents—in January my father got his discharge from the Army Air Forces, in February he and my mother got married, and in April he rejoined Disney's. In-between, they honeymooned in Mexico, and got the inspiration for their take on shirred eggs that they enjoyed at their hotel in Mexico City. Some twenty years later it evolved into a stovetop version that our family always referred to as Special Eggs. You might think so too, perhaps for the flavor and texture of the dish, and certainly for its caloric count. We've updated the ingredients for current tastes. For those who still love all things 1960s and want to try that variation, we're also including the original ingredient list at the end of the recipe. Frankly, the update is better.

Frank & Jeanette's Special Eggs

Ingredients

Makes 4 luxurious soft eggs

* 1 tablespoon butter
* 75–80 cc (>5 tablespoons) heavy cream or half and half
* 4 large eggs (out of the shells, and in individual dishes, if you are on the klutzy side)
* A few drops hot sauce (Tabasco or your preferred)
* A pinch of salt or celery salt (optional)
* 0.8 ounce grated Parmesan cheese

The 1960s' version

* 1 tablespoon margarine
* 1/4 cup or more half and half
* 4 large eggs
* A shake or two of Lawry's seasoned salt
* A few drops of Tabasco sauce
* 2 tablespoons "Parmesan cheese" out of the Kraft green canister

Directions

- Heat butter in a small skillet over medium high heat. You need a pan big enough to hold four eggs comfortably. If it's too small it will make it more difficult to get the finished eggs out. On the other hand, if the pan is too big, it will require more cream and the final product will end up soupy.
- When butter starts foaming, swirl it around, and add cream to the pan.
- Check the depth of cream. Since the point is to poach the eggs gently in warm cream, the cream needs to be about 1/4-inch deep but not so deep that eggs will sink into it. Tricky!
- Turn down the heat to medium and warm the cream gently. Do NOT let it boil.
- Add eggs carefully into the pan.
- Spoon cream over the eggs. The cream should be warm enough to start cooking the egg whites.
- As the egg whites start firming up, quickly dribble hot sauce on top of the yolks.
- Add Parmesan cheese to cover the eggs evenly.
- Cover the pan and cook on low heat for 2 minutes, or longer if you prefer a well-done yolk.
- Turn off the heat. The cream will have thickened and the cheese melted, but the yolks are still soft.
- With a spatula, cut the egg and dairy mass into four pieces and slide out onto plates. Pour any extra thickened cream around the eggs.

Note: This dish makes a great brunch accompanied by cooked greens (something with a little bitterness to balance the richness of the eggs). We like to pair it with sautéed beet greens seasoned with Chinese black vinegar, and a hunk of crusty bread to sop up the goodness. We are pretty sure it will also be spectacular with white toast points (without butter, mind you).

Main Dishes

Robert Lence sampling soup. Moscow, 2017. (Courtesy of Robert Lence.)

Eric Abjornson

Eric Abjornson. (Courtesy of Eric Abjornson.)

Eric was a lead key assistant animator in the 1990s. He worked on films like *Ferngully: The Last Rainforest, Space Jam, Cool World, The Iron Giant,* and *Osmosis Jones.* But in his spare time, Eric studied cooking and attended the California Culinary Institute.

Effects animator Lee Crowe recalled working on *Osmosis Jones*:

> I really enjoyed doing hand drawn effects on that project. It was one of the "partiest" projects I'd worked on in a while. First, there were Eric Abjornson's Friday afternoon fetes, where he'd pull out a convection oven from under his desk, make gourmet hot hors d'oeuvres and serve mixed drinks. But there was also a guy from editorial who would set up a bar, bring martini glasses, gin, vodka, mixers, garnishes, and a shaker and host "Martini Wednesdays." In spite of all that I think we were on time and under budget.

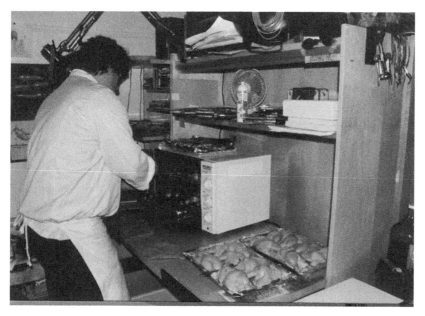

Eric cooking at his animation desk, 1999.

One memorable Halloween, Eric created a haunted cadaver with barbecue ribs for the ribcage, sausages for the guts, frankfurters for fingers, and lots of barbecue sauce for blood. And he still made his drawing quota that week.

Eventually Eric Abjornson left animation to pursue his first love, cooking. Today he is chef at the Ritz Carlton Hotel in Tampa, Florida.

Here is Eric's recipe for London Broil that he used to make for us at his desk:

London Broil

First, you need to prepare a Basic Brine.

Basic Brine

Ingredients

* ❋ 1/2 gallons water
* ❋ 2 tablespoons kosher salt
* ❋ 2 tablespoons brown sugar

This is a basic brine; from this you can expand to whatever you want by just adding your favorite seasonings, spices, herbs, vegetables (garlic!), or juices. (Be careful of citrus as it will "cook" what ever you add it to. Think of ceviche!)

This can be used for any protein. The only difference is the amount of time you let the protein soak in the brine. Here, we are discussing beef.

If you are making fish, you will only need 4–6 hours.

Directions

Chicken: Can go 6 to 24 hours depending on size (i.e., chicken breast would be 4 to 6 hours, a whole chicken(s) can go 12 to 24 based on size.

Beef: Can and should be brined for up to 2 to 3 days depending on cut (i.e., a thick cut, 1 inch plus, can go 3 days or more. 1/2-inch thick or less could go overnight to 2 or 3 days depending the seasonings you want to infuse to the meat).

Special Brine

This particular brine was developed for skirt steak over many years by many chefs. (It can, of course, be used for any beef, pork, or chicken using the previous noted times (be aware that times in brine will vary depending on altitude!)

Ingredients

- 1/2 gallon orange juice
- 1/2 cup soy sauce
- 1/2 cup Worcestershire sauce
- 2 tablespoons kosher salt
- 2 tablespoons brown sugar
- 1 teaspoon Caribbean jerk spice
- 3–4 large garlic cloves

Directions

- Combine all ingredients (except the garlic) till all the salt and brown sugar are dissolved. Add garlic using a microplane or if you don't have a microplane, add a 1/4 portion of the brine and garlic to a blender and pulse to incorporate. Then return to the brine.
- When using beef, allow the beef to soak in the brine for 1 to 3 days. This may take a few times to figure out exactly how much brine you like in your beef. Start with 1 day and add days to it till you figure out how strong you want the flavor to be, usually 2 to 3 days!

Tip: Cut off a good piece of the meat and cook in an oven or pan sear. If the salinity is too strong, then remove the meat form the brine and allow it to soak in clean cold water for 1/2 to 1 hour. Test again. Beef usually needs a bit salt. So adjust to your personal taste.

Cooking London Broil

Directions

- After brining, remove beef from brine and allow to come to room temperature on a covered rack and tray (2–3 hours).
- Grill or sear beef to form a nice crust on each side (depending on previous taste tests, you may want to dust the beef with a bit of salt and pepper or any other seasoning of your using). Then place in an oven, on low side of grill, until an internal temperature of 130°F degrees (using an instant-read, internal-temperature thermometer in the thickest part or the meat for a perfect medium rare).
- Once your beef is cooked to your desired doneness, slice ACROSS the grain, and serve with garlic smashed potatoes and grilled vegetables of the season.

Eric's Halloween Feast for the Warner Bros artists, 1999.

Sergio Aragones

Sergio Aragones has been a master cartoonist for more than 50 years. Sergio's unique pantomime gags in the margins of *Mad* magazine have been a highlight of that publication for decades. His comic book character Groo, co-created with Mark Evanier, has a large fan following. His animation work includes animated gags for the *Mad TV* show (2010–2013), the movie *George of the Jungle* (1997), and *Super Bloopers and Practical Jokes* TV show (1984).

Here is Sergio's mother's recipe for paella in his own words:

Sergio's paella. (Courtesy of Mark Evanier.)

Paella de Dona Isabel

Both my parents were born in Valencia and so was I. As refugees, very few possessions were brought to Mexico, and among them was my grandmother's recipe book.

My best childhood memories were the regular outings to the countryside to cook paella for family and fellow refugees, sometimes 3 or 4 paellas were going at the same time (Valencians' friendly competition) and the kids, always helped, first gathering wood, cleaning shrimp, and, as we grew older, assisting the cook.

In 1962, I emigrated to the United States, started to work for *Mad* and took part in the annual trips organized by its publisher, Bill Gaines. Memorable journeys had been taken to Africa, Haiti, Tahiti, Japan, etc. when Bill asked me to organize the trip to Mexico. The first thing I did was to have my mother, Isabel, cook paella the traditional way…outdoors! This experience of having my American *Mad* family enjoy her cooking and my mother's delight of meeting the men that made her son's career is still one of my fondest memories.

I still cook paella in the same pan and use the same recipe that my mother left me.

The authentic Valencian paella uses snail, rabbit, and no fish. My mother's is a "mixta" (mixed).

Ingredients

* Sofrito (see note below)
* Olive oil to cover the bottom of the paella pan—4 tbsps, or more
* Salt and Pepper to taste
* Pork Loin—1½ lbs cut into 1-inch cubes
* Chicken—1 piece per person. 1 thigh or 1 leg.
* Shrimp—1½ lbs shrimp
* Clams—1 lb
* Mussels—1½ lbs scrubbed, no sand and no hairs
* Garlic—1 clove, minced, per person
* Tomatoes, 3 or 4 large, seeded and finely chopped
* Pimenton (paprika)
* Spanish medium grain rice—½ cup uncooked rice per person
* Water, for cooking the rice
* Clam juice, for cooking the rice when the water evaporates.

* 15 oz can lima beans
* 15 oz can string beans
* 8.5 oz can peas
* Saffron, several strands
* Several sheets of newspaper—to cover pan
* Sweet Pimentos—1 jar.

Sofrito:

* Onion, 1 medium yellow, finely chopped
* Garlic, 2 large cloves, finely chopped
* Green Pepper, 1, finely chopped
* Olive oil, 3 Tbs
* Crushed Tomatoes, 28 oz can
* Paprika, 1 tsp
* 3 bay leaves
* Place all ingredients in the paella pan and cook over a low heat until it has the consistency of jam. This can be done ahead of time.

Directions

* Use a paella pan or flat pan and olive oil to cover the bottom.
* Season (salt & pepper) pork and chicken, cut in 1-inch pieces, two pieces per person.

- Cook until brown (medium heat) and transfer to a platter, add shrimp and cook until almost done and transfer to platter.
- Add the "sofrito" garlic and 3 or 4 tomatoes, seeded and finely chopped; mix well and add a spoonful of "pimeton" sweet paprika and a couple of generous pinches of salt and mix.
- Now add warm water, 2 to 2½ cups per 1 cup of rice (1/2 cup is indicated per person). Check the level of the water, as it will evaporate. I always add clam juice to maintain the water level as it starts boiling, as well as a can of lima beans, another of string beans, and a small one of peas.
- Add the pork and chicken and a couple pinches of saffron. Increase the fire. Check for salt and add the rice. Use fat rice (Bomba or Calasparra from Spain) or Arborio or Blue Rose (California). Never use long-grain thin rice; it won't absorb water. (Make sure it is evenly distributed.)
- When liquid is almost absorbed, add the shrimp, clams, and mussels (no sand, scrubbed and no hairs) and simmer (low fire for about 14 minutes).
- Take out of the fire and cover with newspaper (very important!). Not the comic section—it has color. Let the paella rest for 10 minutes.
- Decorate with strips of sweet pimentos (in jars).
- And do not let your guests serve themselves, they will take all the shrimp!

Sergio's mother Dona Isabel cooking paella outside in the rain, while legendary cartoonist Jack Davis provides cover, 1966. (Courtesy of Sergio Aragones.)

Gus Arriola

Gustavo "Gus" Arriola (1917–2008) was born in Arizona of Mexican parents. He learned English from reading the Sunday newspaper's comics, and his parents moved to Los Angeles when he was 8. After high school, he became an animator and sketch artist for Screen Gems and later at MGM doing *Tom and Jerry*. There he met and married cel painter Mary Frances Servier. During WWII while directing training films, Gus created his comic strip *Gordo*, which made him famous. Although today its stereotype jokes makes one feel uncomfortably un-PC, *Gordo* was the first comic strip that introduced Mexican culture to many average Americans. *Gordo* introduced the public to now popular phrases like, "compadre," "muchacho," and "hasta la vista." Gus even had Gordo cook Mexican cuisine in his comic strip, and printed the recipes. Here is one brought to me by **Hector Cantu,** the co-creator of the comic strip *Baldo*.

Gordo. (Photo by Robert Lence.)

One of the souvenirs I have to share is a recipe for

Gordo's Beans, "Weeth Cheese"

Ingredients

* 2 cups pinto beans (dry)
* 6 cups water
* 1/2 cup shortening or lard

* 1/2 cup chopped cheddar or jack cheese
* Salt

Directions

Cover and simmer beans (in water) slowly 'til tender, about 2½ to 3 hours. (I imagine this means dried beans, not from a can.) Stir often, salting to taste. Pots vary, if necessary to add water before cooking time is up, add boiling water. When done, remove excess liquid, don't drain. Add melted lard. Simmer, uncovered, for half hour, stirring. If too dry, use bit of reserve liquid. Add cheese, cook 'til it melts and serve.

Buen apetito—Gus Arriola

Rasoul Azadani

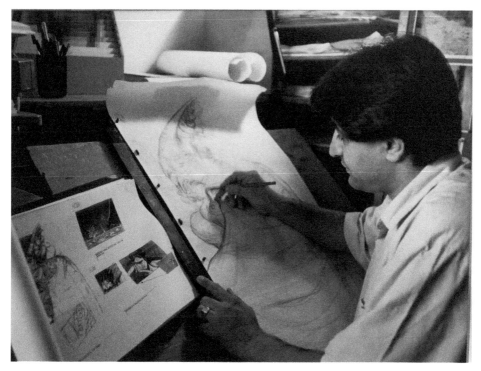

Rasoul Azadani at his desk, 1992. (Courtesy of Arezoo Azadani.)

Rasoul Azadani and his wife **Arezoo** both came to Hollywood from Iran. Rasoul worked at Walt Disney as a layout artist, designer, and animator. His credits include *The Great Mouse Detective, The Little Mermaid, Beauty and the Beast, Aladdin, Pocahontas, Hercules*, and *Moana*.

Here is a recipe they like to make:

Persian saffron rice cakes. (Photo by Arezoo Azadani.)

Tahchin (Persian Saffron Rice Cake)

Serving size: 2 people

Ingredients

* 1 1/2 cup long grain rice
* 1 1/2 cup plain yogurt
* 3 egg yolks
* Saffron (dissolved in 1/4 cup hot water)
* Vegetable oil
* Salt

Directions

- Boil 5 cups of water in a medium-sized pot.
- Add a couple spoons of oil and a spoon of salt to the water.
- Pour the rice into the boiling water and stir occasionally.
- When the rice is cooked on the sides and a little uncooked in the center, empty the rice into a strainer.
- Meanwhile, add yogurt, egg yolks, saffron, and 2 tablespoons of vegetable oil in a bowl and mix them together.
- Slowly add the rice to the yogurt mixture and mix them well.
- Add 2–3 tablespoons of vegetable oil in a nonstick medium-sized pan.
- Pour the rice and yogurt mixture into the pan and flatten the top.
- Put the lid on and let it cook for one hour on a stove top on very low heat.
- After it is done, let it sit to cool off for 10 minutes.
- Place a plate on top of the pan and then flip the pan over. Just like a cake, the rice will land on the plate upside down.

Jane Baer

Jane Shattuck-Takamoto-Baer began her career in the mid-1950s as an animator on Walt Disney's *Sleeping Beauty*. Having worked with many of the Nine Old Men of animation, Jane treasured her work with Marc Davis on Aurora in Sleeping Beauty, and Milt Kahl on Medusa for *The Rescuers*. Later, Jane started an animation studio, Baer Animation, with her then husband Dale Baer, and kept the studio going long after they divorced. In addition to many commercials, feature films, and special projects, Jane supervised the Toontown sequences and Benny the Cab for the legendary film *Who Framed Roger Rabbit?*

This hearty recipe provided a budget dinner for Jane during her Art Center and early days at Disney.

Jane had just started at Disney and moved into her first apartment when she had animators Diane Keener, Stan Green, and Iwo Takamoto over for lunch. A new renter, Jane didn't have any furniture, so they sat on the floor while the group dined on her concoction over a collapsible ironing board. All parties declared their love of Jane's Gobble-Dee-Goop—*or so they said!*

Gobble-Dee-Goop

Ingredients

* 2 1/2 pounds ground beef
* 1 large onion
* 1 bell pepper
* 1 clove of garlic

Directions

* Into a frying pan, stir and brown ground beef, and set aside into a large bean pot.
* Using the same frying pan with the beef drippings, add enough cooking oil to sauté.
* Chop onion, pepper, and garlic together.
* Add chopped veggies to the beef and stir in 3 cans of tomato sauce and 2 cans of pork and beans.
* Pour 1/2 cup of cheap wine (we used Thunderbird) into the empty bean and sauce cans, and stir to collect any remnants from the cans and add the wine to the pot!

- Simmer and stir concoction for 30–40 minutes.
- Salt and pepper to taste. Add ketchup if desired.
- Serve in bowls. Works well with salad and/or garlic bread.

Stuffed Cabbage Rolls

When Jane owned her own studio, there were regular BBQs and potluck lunches, dinners and parties held out on their studio patio. Her cabbage rolls were a regular part of these traditional studio gatherings at Baer Animation.

Ingredients

* 1 pound of raw ground beef
* 1 cup of cooked rice—white or brown
* 1 teaspoon of finely chopped parsley
* 1 egg, unbeaten
* 1/2 cup milk
* 3 teaspoons of minced onion
* 1 teaspoon of salt
* A dash of pepper

* 12 large cabbage leafs
* 2 tablespoons cooking oil
* 1 1/2 teaspoons brown sugar
* 1 can condensed tomato soup
* 1/2 cup of water
* 1 bay leaf
* 3 whole cloves

Directions

Combine ground beef, cooked rice, and parsley. Stir in unbeaten egg and milk. Mix in salt and pepper and only 2 tablespoons of minced onion. Wilt the cabbage leafs by pouring boiling water over them. Drain thoroughly and pat dry. Fill each cabbage leaf with heaping tablespoons of the meat and rice mixture. Fold cabbage leafs over and secure with a toothpick. Place rolls close together in a large baking dish. Sprinkle separately with brown sugar, remaining onion, water, crumbled bay leaf and clove. Cover with tin foil and bake in a moderately slow oven (325°F) for approximately 1½ hours. Add more water, if necessary, as rolls should be nearly covered with water on the sides. Remove the tin foil during the last 15 minutes of baking to allow rolls to brown slightly.

Serve with salads and/or rolls.

Yields about 6 servings.

Depending on the number of artists, recipe can be doubled or tripled, as needed.

Joy Batchelor

John Halas and Joy Batchelor. (Courtesy of Vivien Halas.)

Joy Batchelor (1914–1991) was a British animator, director, and producer. In 1940, she and her husband, John Halas, started Halas & Batchelor Studios in London. For many years, it was the predominant animation studio in Britain. Their most famous collaboration was the film adaptation of George Orwell's *Animal Farm* (1954). Their 1963 film *Automania 2000* was nominated for an Academy Award. In 1967, Joy wrote and directed solo an animated feature of Gilbert & Sullivan's operetta *Ruddigore*.

Here is a reminiscence of her daughter Vivien:

> My mother did most of the cooking on a regular basis. She was a great fan of Elizabeth David, who in the 1950s changed the way people cooked in England by introducing French provincial and Mediterranean food to what had been a rather frugal post-wartime regime. Unlike John, Joy didn't cook the dishes that her mother made such as Shepherds pie or

hash, concoctions made of leftovers, but loved to experiment. She used butter, cream, and wine or vermouth in her recipes and all the things we now avoid…It was very delicious.

Both parents' love of food has been passed on to my brother Paul and me, and Paul's three sons, who are all wonderful cooks.

Veal Casserole

This is the dish we remember:

Ingredients

* ❋ 1 pound of stewing veal, cut into small chunks (from a good butcher)
* ❋ 1 rasher of lean bacon
* ❋ Butter
* ❋ Olive oil
* ❋ 1 clove of garlic
* ❋ Salt
* ❋ Black pepper
* ❋ 1 bay leaf
* ❋ Tarragon
* ❋ Chicken stock
* ❋ 1 leek
* ❋ 1 carrot
* ❋ 1/2 pound of button mushrooms

Directions

- In a frying pan, heat a mixture of olive oil and butter, and quickly sear the veal on all sides.
- Arrange in an earthenware casserole dish that has a tight lid.
- Meanwhile, cook the sliced bacon in the same pan and add to the veal. Pour in a glass of white wine to deglaze the pan and add to the casserole.
- Prepare the carrot and leek, cut into round slices about half an inch thick and add to the casserole along with the fresh tarragon leaves, bay leaf, and a fresh clove of garlic cut into slices.
- Season with salt and black pepper; then cover in water or chicken stock.
- Put the casserole in a hot oven at around 170°C (338°F) for half an hour, and then reduce to around 150°C (302°F) to slow cook the dish for around 2 hours or until the meat is very tender.
- About 30 minutes before serving, add the mushrooms, either sliced or whole if very small.
- Check to taste and allow to rest before serving. If desired, add some crème fraiche right at the end.
- Joy used to serve this dish with green beans and mashed potatoes.

The Happy Cook, by Joy Batchelor. (Courtesy of Vivien Halas.)

Kathryn Beaumont

Disney Legend **Kathryn Beaumont** (the voice of "Alice" from Walt Disney's *Alice in Wonderland*, and "Wendy" from Disney's *Peter Pan*) has the rare distinction of memorable experiences with the mythical worlds of Wonderland and Never Land. Born in England, Kathryn shares this hearty recipe for shepherd's pie, which was a childhood classic she grew up on!

Traditional Shepherd's Pie

Ingredients

* 5 medium russet potatoes
* 1 pound ground beef
* 1/2 cup chopped onion
* 2 teaspoons Worcester sauce
* 1 bouillon cube
* 1/4 cup boiling water

Directions

* Peel, cut, and boil the potatoes. While boiling, sauté onion in a little oil until soft but not browned. Add the beef and continue to sauté, adding salt and pepper to taste, until cooked through. Spoon out the collected fat.
* Add Worcester sauce to the meat. Dissolve bouillon cube in the boiled water, stirring it in also. Place the beef in a 1½ quart casserole dish and set aside.
* Mash the potatoes, adding some butter and milk according to taste, and spoon into the casserole.
* Bake uncovered at 375°F until heated through and browned on top.

Mary Blair

~

Painting for Mary Blair by Roland "Rolly" Crump. (Courtesy of Maggie Richardson.)

Mary Blair (1911–1978), Oklahoma-born Mary Robinson Blair, was one of the top Hollywood animation designers of the mid-twentieth century. Walt Disney once referred to her as "The best artist in the studio." She was married to animation designer Lee Blair, who was younger brother to animator Preston Blair. Some of her films included *Alice in Wonderland* (1951), *Cinderella* (1950), *Peter Pan* (1953), and *How to Succeed in Business Without Really Trying* (1967). Mary was also the designer of *It's a Small World,* the 1964 World's Fair exhibit, that later was relocated to Disneyland.

Mary's niece Maggie Richardson recalled:

> When Mary and Lee were living on the East Coast, we'd visit them and spend some time at their summer place on Lake Winnipesaukee. Lee made rotisserie chicken, and while waiting, Mary would make us a lunch drink she called a **Pink Cow**.

Pink Cow

A **Pink Cow** was ice-chilled borscht with some sour cream whipped in. Just enough to make it her favorite color—shocking pink! She served it with a cucumber stalk. It was great on really hot summer days.

Bruno Bozzetto

Bruno Bozzetto is an award-winning Italian animator and cartoonist. He has produced many famous shorts and feature films including *Allegro Non Troppo* (1976), *West and Soda* (1965), and *VIP My Brother Superman* (1968).

Bruno writes:

Here it is my recipe.

Spaghetti Aglio Olio E Peperoncino

I'm Italian, so it goes without saying that I go crazy for spaghetti.

My favorite recipe is "spaghetti aglio olio e peperoncino" which is a traditional dish in Italy.

It's very easy and quick to make. I usually cook it for my whole family, but here is the recipe for one person.

Directions

- You take a tiny pan and fill it with as many spoons of olive oil as you want in your pasta (usually 4 is more than enough).
- Then, you mince one or two cloves of garlic (remember to take out the core first) and let it cook into the oil along with 2 or 3 peperoncini/chili, or more, depending on how brave you are.
- When the garlic looks golden, it's done. You can pour the oil on spaghetti, "spray" chopped parsley all over it, and finally, if you like, add some parmesan cheese.

Spaghetti aglio olio e peperoncino. (Courtesy of Bruno Bozzetto.)

A hilarious memory: once I went skiing with family and friends. A road accident on the way delayed us and we got to the hotel very late, almost at midnight. We were starving and asked the receptionist if we could have a quick bite. They had no cook available at that time in the night, but decided to be helpful by making spaghetti aglio olio e peperoncino for us. Unfortunately, because the cook was not a cook, they put a ton of garlic in the dish. The day after we realized its terrible effects on our breath! On the cableway. Emptiness had formed all around us ☺.

John Canemaker

John Canemaker. (Photo by Ken Greenwood.)

John Canemaker is an award-winning independent animator, author and historian, who teaches at NYU Tisch School of the Arts. In 2006 he won an Academy Award for his short film *The Moon and the Son, An Imagined Conversation*. (**Note:** Canemaker is the Anglicized version of his original family name, Cannizzaro.)

This is not an old family recipe, but it *is* something quick and easy that I have enjoyed cooking through the years for friends.

Ingredients

* 4 tablespoons extra-virgin olive oil
* 1 large onion, chopped
* 1 long carrot, peeled and cut into thin 1/4-inch rounds
* 2 garlic cloves, peeled and chopped
* 2 cans of Snow's Bumble Bee Chopped Clams in Clam Juice
* 1 cup white wine

* 1/4 teaspoon dried oregano leaves
* Salt and ground pepper to taste
* Juice of 1 lemon
* About 1/2 cup chopped fresh Italian (flat-leaf) parsley
* 2 tablespoons butter, cut in pieces
* 1 pound of linguine

Linguine alle Cannizzaro Clam Sauce

Directions

* Fill a large pot (4–6 quarts) with water and heat to a low rolling boil.
* Add approximately 1 tablespoon salt to the water as it heats.
* Heat a large saucepan at medium-high heat, and add the 4 tablespoons olive oil, coating the bottom.
* Add chopped onion and carrot slices to the hot oil, stirring to coat them well. Lower heat slightly and cook for 3–4 minutes, stirring occasionally, until the onions are soft and translucent.
* Open two cans of chopped clams. Drain off the clam juice and reserve the clams. Pour the clam juice into the saucepan.
* Add chopped garlic cloves, oregano, salt, and ground pepper.
* Add the cup of wine and the lemon juice.
* Bring to a boil and let the mixture cook down a bit, about 5 minutes.
* Meanwhile, cook the linguine in the boiling salted water until al dente, timed per package instructions, and drain.
* Lower the heat on the sauce to a simmer and add the chopped clams, cooking until just heated through, about 3 minutes.
* Remove saucepan from heat and stir in butter pieces and chopped parsley. Mix well.
* Put the linguine into serving bowls and dress with the clam sauce.
* Serve with a dry white wine (Pinot Grigio, Sancerre or Albariño would go well), a simple green salad, and slices of a good baguette.

John Celestri

John Celestri is one of the young animators whose careers were launched by the **Big-Bang** of the Dick Williams' 1977 animated feature film *Raggedy Ann & Andy*. At Nelvana Studios, John became a director and animated the first screen appearance of the Star Wars character Boba Fett the Bounty Hunter. He now creates his young-market comic book series *Snuffy & Zoey's ToyBox Adventures* for the international market.

John Celestri's Real Italian/Brooklyn Spaghetti Sauce (serves 12)

Ingredients

- ✻ 2 28 ounce cans tomato puree (no salt Dei Fratelli)
- ✻ 1 28 ounce can San Marzano peeled plum tomatoes (Cento)
- ✻ 3 large cloves garlic, minced
- ✻ 1 small onion, small dice
- ✻ 1 tablespoon each: fennel seeds, basil, oregano
- ✻ 5 bay leaves
- ✻ 1 tablespoon salt, 1/4 teaspoon black pepper
- ✻ 2 tablespoons sugar
- ✻ 1/4 cup extra-virgin olive oil (or enough to thinly cover bottom of a 3-quart pot)
- ✻ 1/4 pound ground beef
- ✻ 1/4 pound ground pork
- ✻ 1/2 cup grated parmesan cheese
- ✻ 1/2 cup red wine

Cooking Tool: A 3-quart pot (wide-bottomed, 9 inches in diameter is preferable).

Directions

- Empty the plum tomatoes into a large bowl and squash them with your hands.
- In the 3-quart pot, sauté onion and garlic in the olive oil (until the garlic turns golden). Then add the ground beef and ground pork and continue sautéing it all.
- Add all ingredients to the pot and bring it to a boil; then cover, lower the heat, and simmer for 3 hours, stirring occasionally.

Serve on spaghetti with homemade meatballs!

I learned this recipe (and others) from my mother. I wanted to make sure I had several decent meals I could cook for myself when I left home and got my own apartment. Little did I know this spaghetti sauce was the way to a certain girl's heart…I've made this sauce every week since 1979.

Snuffy & Zoey ToyBox Adventures: The Dragon and the Cupcake, 2019. (Copyright John Celestri.)

Virginia Chan

Virginia Chan. (Courtesy of Virginia Chan.)

Hong Kong-born animator **Virginia Chan** was a layout artist for the feature animation *Space Chimps* (2008). She then created a number of online YouTube shorts looking back to the many classic princess movies we all watched growing up and analyze all the crimes, violence, and other legal issues in those movies to see how girls were expected to behave to have their happily ever after. YouTube "Gini Studio" #CrimesInPrincessMovies

From Virgina

My apartment in Pasadena was the central hangout when we were students at USC Animation; we would watch movies and cook. One of my favorite Chinese recipes is dumpling. We had a couple dumpling parties back then where we would make dumplings, eat a couple rounds (of dumplings), and people get to take bags of fresh (raw) dumplings home. Incidentally, I produce cooking videos and publish to the Silas' "You Can Do Anything" Channel on YouTube. The idea is to collect recipes from around the world, over time featuring young chefs making the dish the first time to prove that anyone can learn to cook.

Chinese Dumplings

Wrapping: store bought is easiest but you can also mix equal parts of flour and water, kneel, let rest for 15 minutes, cut in small balls, and roll out to flat circles with a rolling pin.

Filling: Filling could be anything, but my favorite is equal parts of 1) ground pork, 2) mixed veggie (see below), and 3) shrimp. You'll also need 1 egg and seasoning.

This portions are for "mass production" in a party setting.

Ingredients

* Ground Pork—2lbs
* Marinade for Ground Pork—1 1/2 tbsp soy sauce, 1 tsp sugar, 1/2 tsp corn starch
* Napa Cabbage—1 small
* Salt—2 to 3 tbsp
* Chives, 1 bunch
* Salt—1 tsp
* Yellow Chives, 1 small bunch
* Salt—4 tbsp
* Shrimp, 2–3 cups
* White pepper
* Cooking oil
* Egg, 1
* Sesame oil, 1/2 tbsp
* Soy Sauce, 1–2 tbsp
* Wrappers, store bought or homemade
* Small dish of water

Directions

- Ground pork–about 2 pounds–marinade with 1.5 tablespoons soy sauce, 1 teaspoon sugar, 1/2 teaspoon corn starch.
- *Mixed veggie*: chop 1 napa cabbage into small pieces, place in colander, sprinkle salt all over, about 2–3 tablespoons, and let water drain out–about 2 hours (or you can place something heavy on top to force water out to shorten the waiting time).

  Chop chives, 1 bunch, place in small colander, sprinkle salt all over, about 1 teaspoon, again let water drain out.

  Chop yellow chives, 1 small bunch, place in small colander, sprinkle salt all over, about 4 tablespoon, let water drain out.
- *2–3 cups of shrimp*: Remove all shells and head, cut into small pieces, marinate with white pepper and a little cooking oil.

  Mix everything in a large mixing bowl, add 1 egg, 1/2 tablespoon sesame oil, 1–2 tablespoons soy sauce.

  Place 1.5 teaspoon of fillings into one wrapper; have a small dish of water handy to wet the outer edge of the wrapper by running your wet finger on the edge. Close the wrapper by folding in half. There're fancier ways to close it but the main purpose is to close it so it's sealed.

In a pot of boiling water, add dumplings one by one and only as many as one layer spread out in the pot, try not to put dumplings on top of each other as they will stick. When the water boils, add 1/2 cup of cold water, let boil, add another 1/2 cup of cold water. When water boils the third time and the dumpling floats on top of the water, it is done. It is advisable to cook the first 3–4 dumplings and adjust taste before mass producing (add soy sauce if not salty enough, or add egg if too salty).

- *Dipping sauce*: Mix together dark vinegar, soy sauce, sesame oil, and hot sauce.

Chinese Dumplings. (Courtesy of Virginia Chan.)

Chasen's

Chasens restaurant by Tom Sito.

In 1936, Dan Chasen was a vaudeville comic whose career seemed to be sputtering. At the urging of Harold Ross, the editor of *The New Yorker* magazine, and with seed money from movie director Frank Capra, he started his own restaurant. Located in West Hollywood, Chasen's became a hangout for much of the Hollywood film community. Regulars included Alfred Hitchcock, Jimmy Stewart, Ronald Reagan, and Groucho Marx. Humphrey Bogart, Lauren Bacall, and John Huston would meet there to discuss how to fight the Hollywood Blacklist. The drink The Shirley Temple was invented there so little Shirley Temple could enjoy cocktail hour with everyone else.

Walt Disney first met conductor Leopold Stokowski there, and over dinner they began to discuss the idea of doing animation to classical music. This would result in the film *Fantasia*. Many Academy Award after-parties were held there, and in 1982 Disney Studios held the crew party for *The Black Cauldron* there. Chasen's closed in 1994.

Chasen's was best known for its famous chili. Actress Elizabeth Taylor had Chasen's chili flown out to Rome so she could enjoy it on the set of her movie *Cleopatra*. It was also a favorite of Walt Disney. There are many versions of the recipe online. Here is our interpretation.

Chasen's Chili

Ingredients

* 1/2 pound dried pinto beans
* Water
* 1 28-ounce can diced tomatoes in juice
* 1 large green bell pepper, chopped
* 2 tablespoons vegetable oil
* 3 cups onions, coarsely chopped
* 2 cloves garlic, crushed
* 1/2 cup parsley, chopped

* 1/2 cup butter
* 2 pounds beef chuck, coarsely chopped
* 1 pound pork shoulder, coarsely chopped
* 1/3 cup Gebhardt's chili powder
* 1 tablespoon salt
* 1 1/2 tablespoons pepper
* 1 1/2 tablespoons Farmer Brothers ground cumin

Directions

* Rinse the beans, picking out debris. Place beans in a Dutch oven with water to cover. Boil for 2 minutes. Remove from heat. Cover and let stand 1 hour. Drain off liquid.
* Rinse beans again. Add enough fresh water to cover beans. Bring mixture to a boil. Reduce heat and simmer, covered, for 1 hour or until tender.
* Stir in tomatoes and their juice. Simmer 5 minutes. In a large skillet saute bell pepper in oil for 5 minutes. Add onion and cook until tender, stirring frequently. Stir in the garlic and parsley. Add mixture to bean mixture. Using the same skillet, melt the butter and saute beef and pork chuck until browned. Drain. Add to bean mixture along with the chili powder, salt, pepper, and cumin.
* Bring mixture to a boil. Reduce heat. Simmer, covered, for 1 hour. Uncover and cook 30 minutes more or to desired consistency. Chili shouldn't be too thick—it should be somewhat liquid but not runny like soup. Skim off excess fat and serve.
* Makes 10 cups, or 6 main dish servings.

Chasen's used the best beef chuck, center cut, trimmed completely of fat. The restaurant used a special meat grinder, but for the home cook, meat chopped into one-quarter to one-half inch chunks is much better than ground beef for this chili.

Sometimes cumin seed is used in place of the ground cumin. It's a matter of personal preference.

Note: You can freeze this chili for several months. When reheating refrigerated leftover or frozen chili, add a few tablespoons of water to regain proper consistency.

Onil Chibas

New York City native **Onil Chibas** originally studied at Boston University. He then came out to Hollywood and entered animation in production management. He worked at Walt Disney on *Pocahontas* and *The Hunchback of Notre Dame*, then at DreamWorks on *Sinbad* and *Sharktale*. In 1999 he wrote and directed his own short (live action) titled *Grazen*.

By 2003 he had reached a creative crossroads. He felt he needed a change of career direction. So he enrolled himself into the famed culinary academy Le Cordon Bleu, to pursue his other passion, cooking. Today he is a top chef in the Pasadena area. For a number of years he had his own restaurant, Elements, and today has a successful kitchen and catering service.

As a favor to an old animation co-worker (me), here are two recipes of his.

Tuscan Panzanella & Kale Salad with Grilled Chicken Breast

Vinaigrette

Ingredients

* 1/4 cup white balsamic vinegar
* 1/4 cup fresh lemon juice
* 1 tablespoon Dijon mustard
* 1 tablespoon shallot-minced (optional)
* 1 tablespoon kosher salt
* 1 tablespoon of pepper
* 1 1/4 cup olive oil

Directions

* Combine all ingredients except olive oil and mix until salt has dissolved. Whisk in olive oil as you drizzle into vinegar mixture. Adjust seasoning as needed.

Chicken & Marinade

Ingredients

* 2 Chicken breasts skinless, and boneless
* 1/4 cup olive oil
* 3 cloves garlic, smashed and minced

* Zest and juice of 1 lemon
* 1 tablespoon kosher salt
* 1 tablespoon pepper

Directions

* Combine ingredients for the marinade and pour over chicken breasts. Poke chicken with a fork and massage marinade into chicken. Refrigerate for at least 2 hours or overnight.
* Remove chicken from marinade and discard marinade. Grill chicken about 5–7 minutes on each side or until the internal temperature is 155°F on an instant-read thermometer. Remove from grill and set aside to cool. When cool, cut into bite size pieces.

Salad

Ingredients

* 1 loaf (8–12 ounces) of Ciabatta, cut into bite-size pieces
* 1/2 cup olive oil
* 8 ounces kale, ribs removed and cut or torn into small pieces
* 1/2–3/4 pound baby heirloom or other small tomatoes cut in 1/2

* 1/2 red onion, thinly sliced
* 1 bunch of fresh basil, torn into small pieces
* 1/4 cup fresh oregano, roughly chopped
* Sea salt
* Fresh ground pepper

Directions

- Pre heat oven to 375°F. In a large bowl, toss the bread with the olive oil and season lightly with salt and pepper. Spread onto a sheet pan and toast the bread until crisp and lightly browned—check every 5–10 minutes. Remove from oven and cool.
- In a large bowl combine, bread, tomatoes, and red onion. Dress liberally with vinaigrette. Let sit for 15 minutes, allowing the kale to soften and the bread to absorb the dressing. Toss in the basil, oregano, and chicken and combine well. Season salad with salt and pepper to taste.

Cool Sesame Noodle Salad

Dressing

Ingredients

- 1/4 cup rice wine vinegar
- 1/2 cup soy sauce
- 2 tablespoons mirin
- 1/4 cup sesame oil
- 2 tablespoons shallots, minced
- 2 teaspoons garlic, minced
- 2 tablespoons ginger, minced
- 1 tablespoon brown sugar
- 1/4 cup Sambal (chili paste)
- 3/4 cup blended canola /olive oil or other neutral oil
- 2 tablespoons black sesame seeds, toasted

Directions

- Combine all ingredients except neutral oil and sesame seeds and mix until sugar has dissolved. Whisk in neutral oil into soy mixture. Add toasted sesame seeds. Adjust seasoning as needed.

Salad

Ingredients

- 1/2 pound of chow mein noodles
- 2 cups sliced shiitake mushrooms
- 1/2 cup edamame (green soy beans)
- 1 or 2 carrots, julienne or grated
- 1/2 cup + 1/4 cup green onion, cut on bias

- Fresh lemon
- Salt
- Fresh ground pepper

Directions

- Cook noodles according to package directions. Rinse under cool water. Coat them lightly with oil to prevent them from sticking together.
- Sautee shiitake mushrooms in a little oil until they are lightly browned.
- Combine noodles and other ingredients (except 1/4 cup of green onion) in bowl and toss with the dressing. Squeeze a little fresh lemon juice over noodles and season with salt and pepper as necessary. Garnish with reserved 1/4 cup of green onion.

Optional:

You can also add Chinese BBQ pork (purchased from a restaurant) cut into bite size pieces.

Tissa David

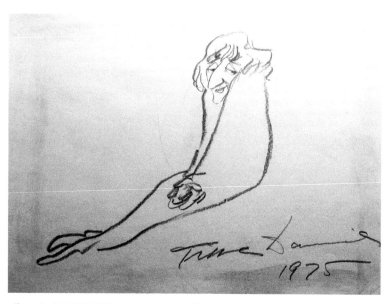

Tissa David self-portrait, 1975. (Courtesy of John Canemaker.)

Teresa "Tissa" David (1921–2012) was not only a great animator, she was a wonderful cook. She grew up in the city of Szeged, in southeastern Hungary. After fleeing her native country in 1950, she lived in Paris for 8 years, where she also mastered French cooking. She settled in New York where she became the dean of NY character animators. Her work graced the films of UPA, John Hubley, Richard Williams, Michael Sporn, and R. O. Blechman. At her cozy Upper East Side apartment, Tissa liked to treat guests to a hometown specialty, Szegediner goulash.

Joe Kennedy, John Canemaker's husband, adapted this from a cookbook called *Hungarian Culinary Art*, by Jószef Venesz, published in Budapest in 1958, embellished with cooking tips from Tissa herself, on how to prepare the sauerkraut for cooking and the importance of using Hungarian paprika.

Szegediner Goulash

Recalled and adapted by Joe Kennedy.

Ingredients

- 1 1/2 pounds boneless pork shoulder
- 1 large sweet onion
- 2 cloves garlic
- 2 pounds bulk sauerkraut—this is important—if you can use fresh sauerkraut, by all means do so. The packaged sauerkraut usually found in the meat or deli section of markets is far preferable to canned.
- 3 tablespoons oil, butter, or lard
- 3 tablespoons paprika—use sweet paprika, not hot or smoked, and if at all possible, get genuine Hungarian paprika—it makes a difference.
- 1 teaspoon caraway seeds (optional)
- 2 cups water
- 1 cup sour cream
- 1 tablespoon all-purpose flour

Directions

- Cut the pork into 1/2-inch cubes. Season well with salt and pepper.
- Slice the onion into thin slices.
- Peel and chop the garlic finely.
- Rinse and drain the sauerkraut. Place in a bowl and fill with cold water, then squeeze the sauerkraut with your hands to remove excess saltiness. Drain in a colander and reserve.
- Heat a Dutch oven or similar heavy-bottomed cooking pot over medium-high heat, and add the butter, oil, or lard.
- When the oil is hot, add the pork cubes in batches and brown, about 5 minutes per side. Add more cooking oil if necessary. Remove browned pork pieces to a bowl and set aside.
- Lower the heat to medium low. Add the onion slices and sauté slowly until they become translucent. Stir in the chopped garlic and paprika.
- Continue cooking down the onion slices, stirring occasionally, for about 20 minutes, until they darken and become caramelized. Take care they do not burn.
- Return the pork cubes to the pot, add optional caraway seeds and 2 cups of water, just enough to cover the meat.
- Bring to a boil, then lower heat and braise the pork for about 30 minutes, partially covered, stirring occasionally. Use a wooden spoon to scrape up any coagulated bits of browned pork from the bottom of the pot.
- Add the rinsed and drained sauerkraut and mix well. Return to a boil, lower heat again, and continue cooking another 30 minutes, or until meat is falling apart.

- Put the sour cream in a bowl and whisk in the flour, mixing well. Then gradually add some cooking stock from the goulash, a few tablespoons at a time, until it is well blended into the sour cream. This tempers the sour cream mixture and helps keep it from curdling.
- Add the tempered sour cream to the goulash, mix well, and simmer everything together a few minutes, until it thickens.

Serve in soup bowls with slices of hearty rustic bread on the side and perhaps a simple green salad. A light white wine, such as a Grüner Veltliner, makes a nice accompaniment.

Alice Davis

Disney legend **Alice Davis** is perhaps best known for her costume designs featured on "It's A Small World" and "Pirates of the Caribbean" rides for Walt Disney's theme parks. A self-proclaimed ranch-cook since the age of 3, Alice quickly became a master chef to please the gourmet palette of her husband, legendary animator Marc Davis. From her vast library of recipes, there were favorite dishes, fascinating drinks, and fine foods always on offer—each with its own story, usually linked to their extensive world travels.

The Davis table often featured bountiful crops of buttery avocados, bananas, and other vegetation from Alice's extensive gardens. To see her in the kitchen was nothing short of a master artist at work! From the swish of a simmering pot to the swing of the oven door, she intuitively knew the exact reach to every spice and treasured tool. The sublime ballet of her preparations was a sight to behold as she conjured up veritable feasts for her guests: "Add just a pinch of this…be sure to try it with that…it's always best with …." Alice is as liberal with her cooking tips as she is with her sage advice, spicy humor, and remarkable acts of kindness. She was, truly, a woman unparalleled.

Here is an improvised dip Alice created for an impromptu gathering many years ago. So successful, it became her go-to dip recipe: simple, but very tasty!

Creamy Salsa Dip

Ingredients

* 1 jar of Pace Thick & Chunky Salsa—choose the desired temperature
* 1 tablespoon of mayonnaise
* 1 pint of sour cream

Directions

- Mix together for desired heat and serve with corn or tortilla chips.
- Prepare 1 day before serving and let it blend for extra flavor.

Ronnie del Carmen

Ronnie del Carmen is an Oscar and Eisner Award-winning cartoonist, writer, production designer, and director who was born in Cavite City in the Philippines. His first work out of school was painting background scenery for Francis Ford Coppola's epic *Apocalypse Now* (1979), which filmed in the Philippines. Ronnie came to the U.S. entering animation doing storyboard work on Warner Bros.' *Batman: The Animated Series,* and later at DreamWorks on *The Prince of Egypt* and *Spirit: Stallion of the Cimarron.* Moving to Pixar, Ronnie has become a senior story supervisor and director on projects like *Finding Nemo, Ratatouille, Up,* and *Wall-E.* He co-directed the film *Inside Out* with Pete Docter, for which he won an Oscar for Best Original Screenplay.

Paper Biscuit by Ronnie del Carmen. (Courtesy of Ronnie del Carmen.)

From Ronnie:

This is my Mom's recipe for *Adobong "Pula"* (tagalog, "Red"). *Adobo* is the emblematic Filipino household dish and though most would quickly add that there are many ways to make it they'll quickly add that theirs is the correct one. The Philippines got adobo from our Spaniard rulers who decided to own the country for over 300 years. It took us a while to get around to kicking them out but we're a hospitable bunch.

Gathering for a meal is standard for Filipino culture in the islands, and we'd feel pretty bad if we can't offer a spread. To not offer at least one home cooked dish or five on your visit for lunch or dinner—announced or unannounced—would haunt the household till they can recover from the transgression with an even larger feast next time.

The Caviteño Pork Adobo "Pula" a la Lilia del Carmen

Ingredients

* Pork tenderloin, pork belly, or shoulder, cubed
* Soak "achuette" (annatto seeds) overnight in 1/2 cup water
* 2 tablespoons of fresh minced garlic
* 2 tablespoons vinegar
* 1 teaspoon peppercorn
* 2 tablespoons soy sauce
* 3–4 bay leaves
* About 3 tablespoons cooking oil

Directions

* Marinate the tenderloin overnight in the vinegar, soy sauce, peppercorn, garlic, and bay leaves. Add 2 cups of water.
* In a medium-sized pot on medium heat, place the pork meat. Save the marinade for after the meat is cooked. Then pour marinade in. Let it cook for 30 minutes.
* Drain the sauce from the pot into a bowl, set aside for later. Cook the meat now till it is dry. Then push the meat to the side. Pour some olive oil and sauté garlic (6 crushed cloves) till brown. Then mix the meat in the sauté. Now we pour the annatto "achuette" soaked sauce. After 5 minutes pour back the sauce you set aside. Let the sauce thicken a bit more. Then you feast!

Caviteño pork adobo. (Courtesy of Ronnie del Carmen.)

Walt Disney

Walt Disney eating barbecue chicken. (Courtesy of The Walt Disney Archives.)

Perhaps no single artist influenced the art of animation so much as **Walter Elias Disney** (1901–1966). He built his small business from a garage into a massive media empire and established new standards for animated feature films, television, and theme parks. It is rare when one single artist can make themselves so synonymous with their artform.

Walt Disney had a humble background. He was raised on a farm and had to go to work at an early age to help the family. He dropped out of high school to join the army for World War I. But while some other famous film artists like Orson Welles and Charlie Chaplin overcompensated for their poor beginnings by developing elite gourmet tastes, Walt never lost his working class roots when it came to food. When working late, he was known to skip lunch and munch a few cold hot dogs out of the fridge while working. Most of all, Walt Disney loved chili. He loved chili from Chasen's of Beverly Hills, or chili out of a supermarket can. When traveling and working abroad, he'd have his chili flown for him to eat in his hotel room or office.

This is his personal recipe.

Walt's Personal Chili

Ingredients

Chili

* 2 pounds coarse ground beef
* 2 onions, sliced
* 2 cloves garlic
* 1/2 cup oil
* 1 cup chopped celery
* 1 teaspoon chili powder (depending on taste)
* 1 teaspoon paprika
* 1 teaspoon dry mustard
* 1 large can solid pack tomatoes
* 2 pounds dry pink beans
* Salt

For Extra Zest

Add a pinch of the following spices:

* 1 little yellow Mexican chili pepper
* Coriander seeds
* Turmeric
* Chili seeds
* Cumin seeds
* Fennel seeds
* Cloves
* Cinnamon
* Dry ginger

Directions

Soak beans overnight in cold water. Drain, add water to cover (2 inches over beans), and simmer with onions until tender (about 4 hours). Meanwhile, prepare sauce by browning meat and minced garlic in oil. Add remaining ingredients, and simmer for 1 hour. When beans are tender, add sauce to beans and simmer for 1/2 hour. Serves 6–8.

Walt Disney having lunch with Max Fleischer, 1954. L-R Gerry Geronimi, Walt Disney, Ben Sharpsteen, Ted Sears, Max Fleischer, Dick Huemer, George Stalling, Richard Fleischer, Andy Engman, Wilfred Jackson. (Courtesy of the Margaret Herrick Film Archives.)

Pete Docter

Minnesota native **Pete Docter** was one of the first animators hired for the young company called Pixar right out of graduating Cal Arts in 1990. He became a key creative member of the group known as "The Brain Trust" there. He did animation, storyboards, screenwriting, and directing. He is best know for the classic films *Monsters, Inc., Inside Out,* and *Up.*

In 2018, Pete Docter was named overall creative head of Pixar Studio.

Here is Pete's recipe, in his own words.

Basil Pesto Pasta

Ingredients

* Basil Leaves 3 cups
* Romano Cheese 1/2 cup grated
* Olive oil 1/2 cup
* Pine nuts 1/3 cup
* Garlic 3 cloves
* Salt
* Fettucini one package

Optional:

* Petit potatoes
* Green beans
* Snap Peas
* Corn
* Chicken, cooked, cubed

Directions

* First, make the PESTO: 3 cups fresh basil leaves 1/2 cup freshly grated Romano or Parmesan-Reggiano cheese 1/2 cup extra virgin olive oil 1/3 cup pine nuts 3 garlic cloves Salt to taste Pop it all in the food processor. Add more olive oil as needed to make the mixture liquid. (Any unused pesto can be frozen; we freeze ours in an ice cube tray for easy use later.) FETUCCINI: Follow instructions for amount and preparation on package. From there, add some variation of the following, depending on what you like: Petite potatoes, boiled Green Beans, steamed Snap Peas, steamed Fresh corn, steamed; kernels cut off husk Chicken, cooked, cubed.

It's all pretty freeform, depending on what's fresh or what you like. Toss them all in a big bowl with salt and pepper. Garnish with a sprig of basil and enjoy!

Friz Freleng

Friz Freleng. (Courtesy of Hope Freleng-Shaw.)

Isadore "Friz" Freleng (1906–1995) came to Hollywood from Kansas City with the first group of Disney animators. After awhile he left Walt and helped start Leon Schlesinger's Looney Tunes Studio. Friz was one of the most iconic Warner Bros. cartoon directors in their Golden Age. He directed some of the best work of Porky, Bugs, Tweety, Sylvester, and Yosemite Sam. Legend has it Yosemite Sam was modeled on Friz, in part when he would lose his temper at the moviola, stomp his feet, and exclaim, "OOOHHH!!!"

Friz Freleng won five Academy Awards and three Emmys. After Warner's animation unit closed, Friz started DePatie-Freleng and created the successful *Pink Panther* and *Ant and the Aardvark* series.

This recipe is a reminiscence of his daughter Hope Freleng-Shaw:

Matzoh ball soup. (Photo by Robert Lence.)

Lily Freleng's Matzo Balls

Friz Freleng's Favorite

Ingredients

* 4 extra large eggs
* 1 teaspoon salt
* 1 cup matzo meal (Manischewitz)
* 1/4 cup ice water
* 3 tablespoons chicken fat (I guess today you would use vegetable oil, but chicken fat makes them the best)

Note: Rendered chicken fat can be found in many kosher markets.

Directions

Beat eggs and salt together. Add matzo meal. Then add ice water, and then melted chicken fat. Put in refrigerator, covered well. Refrigerate at least 2 hours or longer. Bring a large pot of salted water to a boil over medium heat. Wet hands with cold water. Roll matzo meal mixture into balls, golf ball size or a little bigger. Put into boiling water, cover pot. Reduce heat to simmer, but light boil for 25 minutes. Do not peek! Remove with slotted spoon into chicken soup.

Lily Freleng's Chicken Soup with her Wonderful Matzo Balls

Ingredients

* One whole chicken (fryer) cut into 1/8th parts
* One bunch of small carrots (they are sweeter)
* 6 celery sticks (tops off)
* 2 brown onions (skins off)
* 1 parsnip
* 1 turnip
* 1 teaspoon salt
* 2 teaspoons fresh parsley (chopped very fine)
* 2 tablespoons chicken granules

Directions

* Wash chicken in cold water.
* Start with a large soup pot of cold water. Add clean chicken to cold water.
* Start at low boil and keep skimming off the brown foam that comes to the top with a slotted spoon, until there is no fat or foam left.
* Turn down to simmer for 30 minutes. Keep skimming if necessary, to clear the broth.
* Add onions, parsnip, and turnip. (They take the longest to cook.)
* Cook on low/medium heat for 45 minutes.
* Add in celery and carrots. (I cut celery in half, tops off carrots, but whole.)
* Let cook at low boil, with top off, for 2 hours.
* Add salt and pepper to taste.
* Add chicken granules after tasting, if it needs more flavor.
* Add chopped parsley, last 20 minutes (only for color).
* I take top off soup last 30 minutes to thicken, if needed.
* Serve soup with matzo ball, carrot, and celery only.
* Can add chicken pieces if you like.

This soup gets more rave reviews then any other chicken soup I know of.

Shhh, secret recipe!

A Recipe for Marriage from Lily and Friz Freleng, from 1932.

- First you start with a young, vivacious woman.
- Add a handsome, outgoing man.
- With a lot of talent.
- Then, add a lot of love.
- Delicately sprinkle with affection.
- After waiting a minute, add a dash of humor, and a tablespoon of understanding.
- Mix vigorously.
- Put some schmaltz in it, and it will add a golden richness, a bubbling warmth, a loving tenderness, a promise of good things to come. Of course, some people will say that putting schmaltz in it is hamming it up. They should bite their tongues.
- Then stir in ability to forgive and lots of compassion.
- Keep adding various spices to keep interesting flavor throughout a lifetime.
- Bake for many long and exciting years.
- Result? A long and happy relationship, and everlasting marriage.

Raul Garcia-Sanz

Raul Garcia-Sanz is a Spanish animator who has worked extensively around the world. Raul's talents have contributed to classics like *Lucky Luke* for Hanna and Barbera, Don Bluth's *Land Before Time*, Walt Disney's *Who Framed Roger Rabbit*, *The Lion King*, and *Tarzan*. He has created and animated his own films, such as his homage to the stories of Edgar Allen Poe, *Extraordinary Tales* (2013).

Raul and his journalist wife, Rocio Ayuso, are both natives of Madrid, who have settled in Hollywood. There they cook the cuisine of their native land for their friends.

Here is Rocio:

Tortilla De Patatas

(Spanish omelette)

With more and more Spanish professionals in the animation world, a tortilla de patatas has to be included. It's a must in any Spanish reunion: tapas or main dish, warm or cold. It is now also considered a trending vegetarian dish!

Ingredients

* 5 potatoes
* 1 onion
* 6 eggs
* Olive oil (10 ounces)
* A pinch of salt

Directions

* Peel potatoes and cut them on uneven slices. Peel and cut the onion in small pieces. Mix them both with salt. Put the olive oil in a pan. It should be almost two fingers deep over medium heat. Add half the onion and potatoes mix when oil is hot. Let it all simmer in the oil on medium to low heat. You are not frying them, you want them soft. While cooking, cut and move them a little with a fish slice. Remove the first bunch when you see them golden (not brown) and semi soft. Repeat with the rest of the potatoes.

- Crack the eggs into a mixing bowl. Add the potatoes and onion already cooked to the battered eggs. Potatoes and onions should be with as little oil as possible. Mix them well in a bowl and let it settle together for few minutes.
- Remove most of the oil from the pan, leaving it just greasy.
- Place the pan back over low heat. Transfer the mixture evenly on the pan.
- Cook it slowly till there's almost no runny egg on top moving the pan softly so it doesn't get stuck. Cover the pan with a dinner plate or a flat lid of the same size. Carefully but decisively flip the pan over the dinner plate and slide the omelette back into the pan to cook the other side for another 5 minutes till golden or till desired. Slide it (or flip it) into the serving plate and voila!

Serving methods

Cut in squares (like Hellraiser face) to serve as tapas.

Cut in 4 to 6 wedges to serve as main dish (for 4–6) with a green salad. Roasted pepper salad is very good too.

Can also be served with mayo on the side.

Save a piece for the next day with your coffee to be a real Spaniard!

Michael Giacchino

Michael Giacchino. (Photo by Andy Paradise.)

Michael Giacchino began by doing stop-motion animation of a character timed to music in his basement in Riverside, New Jersey. He studied animation and production at the School of Visual Arts in New York, but saw he had a knack for writing music. After courses at Julliard and an internship at Universal Studios, Michael embarked on career as one of the foremost composers of movie scores today. He created the distinctive music for such hits as Brad Bird's *The Incredibles* (2004) and *Incredibles 2* (2018), *Ratatouille* (2007), *Zootopia* (2016), *Inside Out* (2015), and *Coco* (2017). In addition to films like J. J. Abrams' *Star Trek* (2009), and *Star Wars: Rogue One*, and video games like *Medal of Honor: Airborne* (2007). He won an Oscar for the score of *Up* (2009).

Michael's Best

(Named by my children and their friends.)

This recipe came out of the necessity to cook up something fast that the kids would like for dinner on busy days.

Ingredients

* 1 pound of penne or rigatoni pasta (fresh or homemade is always best!)
* 1½ cup of grated parmesan cheese
* 1–2 egg(s), room temperature if you have the time (If you plan ahead, eggs at room temperature are a good idea.)
* 12 ounces of diced pancetta
* Salt
* Butter
* Optional extras: chopped olives, sun dried tomatoes

Directions

* Sauté the diced pancetta (plus any extras) in a small amount of olive oil while boiling the water for the pasta in a separate pot.
* Use this time to prepare your eggs and parmesan cheese and have them at the ready. Note on the eggs: I crack them right into the pasta (see below) but some people like to whisk ahead of time. Either way is fine!
* After the pasta is cooked and removed from the water, *immediately* break the eggs and put the pancetta, eggs and the grated parmesan cheese in with the cooked pasta and stir very well so that the heat from the cooked pasta cooks the eggs as you stir. The more you stir the creamier the texture will become. Add salt as needed— however my father has always said that "as soon as you think you may have put too much salt in—put in a little bit more!"

After a minute or two you should be good to go! Start serving and enjoy!

Oscar Grillo

Illustration by Oscar Grillo. (Courtesy of Oscar Grillo.)

Illustrator and animator **Oscar Grillo** has been working in animation since 1960. After a stint at Richard William's Animation Studio in London, he formed Dragon Pictures with Geoff Dunbar, and later Klacto Pictures with Ted Rockley. Oscar designed and animated a number of award-winning commercials and shorts, most notably the BAFTA winning *Seaside Woman* (1980), based on the song by Paul and Linda McCartney. He also contributed to the films *Men in Black* (1997) and *Monsters, Inc.* (2001).

Although long-time residents of London, Oscar and his wife Pat retain strong cultural ties to their native Argentina. Here is one of their recipes.

Empanadas Argentinas

For the pastry:

Ingredients

* 500 g plain white flour
* 220 g vegetable lard
* 260 ml salty water (warm but not hot)
* 2 teaspoons baking powder

Directions

Place the flour in a large bowl with the baking powder. Mix in the lard and gradually add enough salty water to make uniform and elastic dough. Leave to rest for about 1 hour or until the filling is ready, then roll out to about 0.70 cm thickness and cut into 14-cm circles.

For the filling:

Ingredients

* 150 ml olive oil
* 500 g lean beef ground or cut by hand into very small pieces
* Two medium or one very large onion, chopped
* 200 g chopped tomatoes
* 3 garlic cloves
* 1 teaspoon cumin
* Mild, dry red pepper flakes or paprika
* 2 hard-boiled eggs, sliced, and 1 beaten egg for brushing on
* 2 cups of green olives, chopped into large pieces
* 1 cup sultanas or raisins previously re-hydrated in water and drained
* Salt and pepper

Directions

* Heat the oil in a medium-size pan and fry the chopped onions until soft, then add the beef and stir around to brown it, add the tinned tomatoes, chopped garlic, cumin, dry red pepper or paprika, salt, and pepper and cook for 10 or 15 minutes on a low heat, stirring occasionally. Add the drained sultanas or raisins and the pieces of green olives and leave to cool.

- Place 1–2 tablespoons of the beef in the centre of each pastry circle and add a slice of hard-boiled egg on top. Fold the pastry in half over the filling and seal the edge by crimping or making a "repulgue." (Search online for instructions.)
- Place the empanadas on a baking tray lined with greaseproof paper and brush them with beaten egg to give them colour. Bake at 200°C in a preheated oven for about 8–9 minutes or until golden. The pastry can be bought as disks from stockists of Argentinean foods or ready-made puff pastry can be used.

Chimichurri

This is a sauce Argentineans use as a complement to barbecued meats. It can also be used to marinade the meat before grilling.

It is easy to make and bears no resemblance to any bought chimichurri, which is made with dried herbs and preservatives. Always use fresh ingredients and good virgin olive oil.

Ingredients

- A large bunch of fresh, preferably flat, parsley
- Several garlic cloves, according to taste
- One large green pepper
- Enough olive oil to cover the chopped ingredients
- A splash of wine vinegar, to taste
- A handful of dry red pepper flakes, to taste, hot or mild according to preference
- Salt and pepper

Directions

Chop the ingredients finely, by hand or in a food processor. Add the oil and vinegar to taste, until you achieve a consistency of a green sauce, neither too liquid nor too dry. It lasts several days in the fridge.

John Halas

Joy Batchelor and John Halas cooking together, 1947. (Courtesy of Vivien Halas.)

John Halas (1912–1995) learned animation in Hungary before moving to England in 1936. In 1940, John and his British animator-bride Joy Batchelor started Halas & Batchelor Studios in London. For many years it was the predominant animation studio in Britain. Their most famous collaboration was the film adaptation of George Orwell's *Animal Farm* (1954). They also created 70 short films, commercials, and educational films. John co-wrote *Techniques in Film Animation*, and *Timing for Animation*, seminal books in animation education.

Here is a memory from his daughter Vivien:

Hungarian Chicken Soup "Ujhazy Tyukleves"

As you know, John was Hungarian, and from time to time he used to make meals that his Jewish mother used to cook, such as chicken paprika and gulyas stew. But his all-time favorite was "Ujhazy tyukleves," a traditional chicken soup where you have the broth as a soup and then eat the chicken and vegetables separately. In those days chicken was a great luxury and all free range. Sometimes he would serve it with the chicken shredded in the soup and with noodles, so in other words a chicken noodle soup.

This is how he made it as I remember.

Ingredients

* 1 free-range chicken
* 1 small onion, sliced
* 2 hearts of celery
* 1 carrot
* 1 parsnip

* 100 g (3½ ounces) of mushrooms
* Salt
* Peppercorns
* Parsley
* Ginger

Directions

* Put the whole chicken in a large casserole with the sliced onion.
* Add water and bring to a boil; skim off any scum.
* When the chicken is half cooked, add the vegetables that you have cut lengthways.
* Add salt to taste.
* Add the parsley, peppercorns, and ginger in a muslin bag.
* Put the casserole back on the stove top covered by a tight lid, and allow to simmer until the meat is very tender.
* Serve the soup first with noodles and the chicken separately with the vegetables.

William Hanna

Bill Hanna. (Courtesy of the Hanna Family.)

William Hanna (1910–2001) was born in New Mexico. In 1937, at MGM, he teamed with New Yorker Joseph Barbera (1911–2006) to form one of the greatest collaborations in Hollywood. First they directed the *Tom and Jerry* series of award-winning animated shorts. In 1957 they formed Hanna-Barbera Productions, for many years the largest animation studio in the business. They created famous shows like *The Flintstones, The Jetsons, Scooby Doo*, and earned 7 Oscars and 8 Emmy awards.

This is from Bill Hanna's son and daughter-in-law Dave and Ginny:

Bill Hanna and his wife, Violet, loved the Fall River Valley in Shasta County (Northern California) that they were introduced to in the late 1940s and ultimately built a vacation home there in the 1980s. The area is known for being producers of wild rice. Bill loved the outdoors, so I have taken the liberty of attaching a picture of Bill from one of his many successful fishing expeditions.

Bill and Violet enjoyed this easy-to-make wild rice casserole, sometimes substituting chicken for beef.

Wild Rice Casserole

Serves 6

Ingredients

- 1 cup Fall River Wild Rice
- 3 cups boiling water
- 1 pound ground beef
- 1 4-ounce can mushrooms

- 3 tablespoons chopped onion
- 2 cans chicken broth
- 1 bay leaf
- Salt, pepper, garlic salt, paprika to taste

Directions

Boil water; remove from stove. Add rice and let soak for 15 minutes. Sauté onion, mushrooms, and ground beef. Mix all ingredients in large casserole dish. Refrigerate up to 1 day if desired. 1 1/2 hours prior to serving, add 1 cup water. Cover casserole and bake 1 hour at 375°F. Uncover and bake 1/2 hour longer.

Yvette Kaplan

Yvette Kaplan was born in New York City. Her credits include *Beavis and Butthead Do America, Ice Age, Arthurs Missing Pal, Doug, Ducktales,* and *Zack & Quack,* for which she is the creator.

Here is her own recipe:

Dandelion and Grapefruit Salad

Ingredients

* 1 bunch (11 ounces) dandelion greens, ends trimmed, leaves torn
* 1 large pink grapefruit peeled and segmented; squeeze remaining membrane and save juice for dressing
* 1/2 cup sliced red onion
* 1/2 cup pomegranate seeds
* 1 teaspoon Dijon mustard
* 1 tablespoon honey
* 3 tablespoons apple cider vinegar
* 2 tablespoons extra-virgin olive oil
* 1/2 teaspoon sea salt
* 1/2 teaspoon pepper

Directions

* Put greens, grapefruit segments, onion, and pomegranate seeds in a bowl.
* Mix grapefruit juice, mustard, honey, vinegar, oil, salt, and pepper together in a small bowl.
* Pour half the dressing over salad and toss gently to combine.
* Serve remaining dressing on the side.

Mark Kausler

Mark Kausler and Cathy Hill.

Mark Kausler is an animator originally from Kansas City. Since starting on *The Yellow Submarine* in 1968, Mark animated *The Maybelline Seq.* from Ralph Bakshi's *Heavy Traffic*, as well as *Who Framed Roger Rabbit, The Duck Factory, The Lion King, Beauty and the Beast*, and the premiere episodes of *Ren & Stimpy* and *The Rugrats*.

Mark is also one of the great archivists of animation history. There is almost no book on animation that does not owe some of its research to Mark's consultation.

Summer Spaghetti

Recipe by Mark Kausler and Cathy Hill

Cook Pasta (Spaghetti)

Ingredients

* Spaghetti, 1 lb. cooked
* Tomatoes, 4–6 finely chopped
* Green Onions, 3 finely chopped
* Lemon Juice, 1 TB
* Vinegar, 1 TB
* Olive Oil, 3 or 4 TB or more

* Basil, 3tbs fresh or 1 ½ tbs dried
* Salt and Pepper to taste

Optional:

* Sausage, fried and crumbled (pork or vegan)

Directions

Combine the lemon juice, vinegar, olive oil and basil to make a dressing. Toss the spaghetti, tomatoes and green onions in a large pasta bowl. Add the dressing and mix thoroughly.

SIMPLE, SIMPLE, SIMPLE

GOOD, GOOD, GOOD

"Frogs' Legs," drawing by Cathy Hill.

Glen Keane

Linda and Glen Keane with Tom and Pat Sito celebrating his 2018 Oscar for the short film *Dear Basketball*.

Glen Keane is one of the great animation artists of our time. Since he entered Walt Disney Studios in 1974, his superb draftsmanship has given life to many of Disney's most beloved characters: Ariel, the Little Mermaid, Beast in *Beauty and the Beast*, Pocahontas, Rapunzel from *Tangled*, and many more. Since leaving Disney he has won an Oscar for his short film *Dear Basketball*, written by NBA legend Kobe Bryant.

In Glen's life, art has always been a family affair. His father, Bill Keane, created the famous comic strip *The Family Circus*, which was later taken over by his brother Jeff. His children, Claire and Max, have both gone on to successful careers in filmmaking.

> For me, drawing is the greatest joy. Animation is never as good as when I'm sitting at that desk drawing. Even when it's up on the screen, it's never as wonderful as those moments when it's drawn, to me.

— Glen Keane

In the Keane Family, cooking is also a family affair. Glen's wife, Linda, sent me this great recipe with the note: "Glen requested I send our Swedish meatball recipe, which is our traditional Christmas dinner. And he is good at making them (with a little help)."

Swedish Meatballs

Ingredients

- 1 pound lean ground beef
- 1/2 pound lean ground pork
- 1 cup fresh breadcrumbs (3 slices)
- 1/2 cup whole milk
- 1/4 cup minced onion or grated
- 1 clove garlic, minced
- 1 egg
- 1 teaspoon salt
- 1/2 teaspoon white pepper
- 1/4 teaspoon allspice (to taste)
- 1/4 teaspoon nutmeg (to taste)
- Gravy (for a whole batch; reduce amounts if cooking fewer meatballs)
- 4 tablespoons butter, divided
- 3 tablespoons flour
- 3 cups chicken or beef broth
- 1/4 cup heavy whipping cream

Directions

- Combine all meatball ingredients in the bowl of a stand mixer. Mix with paddle attachment until very smooth. Alternatively, mix by hand until smooth.
- Form into about 40 1-inch balls and arrange on waxed paper-lined baking tray. Chill 30 minutes. (Or freeze until solid, and then pack into airtight containers to save for another meal. Do not thaw before cooking; add an extra 5–10 minutes cook time.)
- Melt 2 tablespoons butter over medium-high in a large skillet and fry half the meatballs, turning frequently, until browned. They should not be cooked through at this point. Remove.
- Add remaining butter and cook rest of meatballs the same way. Remove.
- Add flour to skillet and whisk to cook until toasted.
- Whisk in stock until smooth.
- Add meatballs back to skillet and stir gently to coat in gravy. Simmer 10–15 minutes until thickened and meatballs are cooked through.
- Turn heat to low and gently stir in cream.
- Serve over egg noodles, mashed potatoes, or rice.

Ward Kimball

Ward Kimball (1914–2002), originally from Minneapolis, was one of Walt Disney's great animation team, The Nine Old Men. He breathed life into characters like Jiminy Cricket, Pecos Bill, The Mad Hatter, Lucifer the cat, Bacchus in the Pastoral from *Fantasia*, and the pearly band in *Mary Poppins*. Ward directed two Oscar-winning shorts, *Toot Whistle, Plunk and Boom* and *Its Tough to be a Bird*.

He organized and led the animation team for the *Disneyland* TV Show, as well as playing trombone in the animators' jazz combo, the Firehouse Five Plus 2. His enthusiasm for collecting model railroad trains influenced Walt Disney in his own collecting and building of model trains. This ultimately led to the creation of Disneyland.

This reminiscence is from Ward's son, animator John Kimball, whose own career includes films like *The Adventures of Raggedy Ann & Andy* and the first *Star Trek* movie, and TV series like *Darkwing Duck, Marsupilami, Chip & Dale's Rescue Rangers, Bonkers*, and *Goof Troop*.

Hash with Peanuts and Fuyu Persimmons

Ward rarely cooked, other than barbecue. Once, when our mother was gone and Ward had to take care of my sisters and me, he created the dish for which he is infamous: Pour canned chili & beans into a saucepan, add shelled peanuts, heat and serve. Voila!

On a completely different note, and decades later, Ward created a real masterpiece from their garden, often served at Thanksgiving or other festive dinners in fall. This is good as an appetizer or side dish:

Ingredients and Directions

* Slice Fuyu persimmons like a tomato, discarding stems, and arrange on a platter, preferably turquoise in color.
* Squeeze fresh lime juice over the persimmons.
* Scatter pomegranate seeds on top, and serve.

Bon Appetit!

Bill Kroyer

Bill Kroyer worked on *The Fox and the Hound*, *Animalympics*, and *Tron*, and he won an Oscar nomination in 1987 for *Technological Threat*. Together with his wife, Sue, they both created the film *Ferngully the Last Rainforest* (1992).

"Chinese" Pancakes

From Bill Kroyer:

This recipe has been in my family for over 50 years and was taught to me by my Aunt Marion. Why was it called "Chinese" pancakes? She never explained that, but I joked with her that they should have been called "Nationalist Chinese" pancakes, because (stay with me) to prevent the dough from collapsing you were not supposed to open the oven door to look at it; in other words: "No Peking* (peeking)."

Setting aside that dodgy origin, they are delicious and hold a special place in my personal animation history. When I was a young Disney animator, I invited one of my co-workers to my tiny house in Hollywood and made her Chinese pancakes. She was so impressed she agreed to a first date. Thus began the courtship that led to my 40-year (and counting) marriage to the Incredible Sue Kroyer.

Ingredients	
❄ 2 eggs	❄ 1/2 cup white flour
❄ 1/2 cup milk	❄ 3 teaspoons butter

Directions

- The key to this recipe is a tempered 8-inch IRON SKILLET. If you don't have one, don't attempt this recipe!
- Set oven at 350°F. Put the butter in the skillet and place it in the oven.
- Whisk together the eggs and milk. Gradually whisk in the flour. Use a whipping action to aerate the mixture. By the time the batter is smooth, the skillet should be hot, with the butter melted. Swirl the skillet so the butter coats the bottom and sides of the skillet. Pour the mixture into the center so it spreads evenly in the skillet. Carefully place the skillet back in the oven. Bake (without peeking) 20 minutes.
- It should puff up and brown beautifully! Serve with powder sugar or maple syrup.

Note: You can double this recipe if you have a larger iron skillet.

---

* Peking was an old name for the Chinese capitol Beijing.

Sue Kroyer

Animator **Sue Kroyer** worked for Richard Williams Studios on *Raggedy Ann & Andy,* on Don Bluths *Banjo the Woodpile Cat,* and on Brad Bird's *Family Dog* and *The Iron Giant.* At Walt Disney she worked on *The Fox and the Hound* and *The Black Cauldron.* With her husband, animator Bill Kroyer, they created the film *Ferngully the Last Rainforest* (1992).

In 2016 Sue and Bill were awarded the June Foray Award by ASIFA/Hollywood.

Schmoos

History: SCHMOOS is an Americanized traditional Danish dish. My Wisconsin parents, Bud and Jean Nelson, renamed the Danish dish after the characters in the Al Capp comic *Lil' Abner.* Schmoos were lovable creatures who wanted to be eaten! They were incredibly popular in the 1950s. Pork is a traditional Danish dish, and this has been a family favorite as long as I can remember. Until now, the recipe has never been written down.

Serves 4

Ingredients

* 1 pork tenderloin (trimmed to remove silver skin; can be removed by a butcher)
* 6 eggs
* 72 crushed RITZ crackers
* 4 small cans Campbell's Cream of Mushroom soup (*not* non-fat!)
* 2T butter
* 1/2 cup vegetable oil

Directions

* Preheat oven to 325°F
* Trim, wash, and pat dry the pork tenderloin.
* On cutting board, slice pork into 1/2-inch slices.
* Using a meat tenderizer, pound each slice of pork almost flat.
    (About 1/4-inch high—piece will double in diameter)
* Crush RITZ crackers into crumbs. Place 2 cups into a shallow bowl.
    (You will need to keep re-stocking this bowl.)

- Crack eggs into another shallow bowl and beat with a fork.
- In a large, nonstick skillet, melt 1 tablespoon of butter with 1/4 cup vegetable oil.
- Heat pan to medium-high heat.
    (Temperature is tricky—warm enough to sauté and brown the meat, but not burn.)
- In a Dutch oven or covered casserole dish, spread a layer of soup on the bottom with a spoon.

To Cook

- Start with 3–4 medallions at a time (as many as will fit in the pan).
- Dip each pork slice into beaten egg mixture, shake off excess egg.
- Then dredge medallion into crumbs, turn, coating completely.
- Place coated medallion into hot oil. Saute until golden brown on both sides.
    (Be careful not to burn!)
- Place medallions on the bottom of the casserole dish (as many needed to cover the bottom of dish).
- Place one heaping tablespoon of soup on top of each medallion. Spread with the bottom of the spoon to cover each medallion.
- REPEAT process until all medallions are sautéed and layered in the dish.
    (on each layer, overlap the slices—cover the gaps—rather than stack directly on top of each other.
- Finish with a layer of soup on top.
- Cover, bake for 1 hour 45 minutes at 325°F.
- Let sit for 10 minutes before serving.

Traditional side dishes

Boiled, quartered red potatoes; boiled sliced carrots; and French-style green beans.

Candy Kugel

Collage by Candy Kugel, featuring Vincent Cafarelli. (Courtesy of Buzzco Assoc. Inc.)

Candy Kugel began at Perpetual Motion Pictures in New York doing political cartoons for NBC, ads, and TV specials. Later she and partner Vincent Cafarelli became the creative force behind Buzzco Associates. There they did commercials and educational films, notably MTV's initial launch campaign, Planned Parenthood's "Talking About Sex," and WGBH Emmy-winning *Between the Lions*. Candy remains a strong voice for New York's independent animation community. And every year, Candy hosts a Passover Seder for 28!

Passover Charoset

Food I make one time a year, but yummy enough to eat every day:

Charoset (for a large crowd)

This is the traditional sweet spread representing the mortar used by Hebrew slaves.

Ingredients

* 12 firm apples
* Lemon juice
* 1 cup chopped walnuts
* 1/2 cup pitted dates, chopped
* 1/2 cup dried apricots, chopped
* 1/2 cup slivered almonds
* 1/2 cup raisins
* 1/2 cup dried figs, chopped
* 1 cup honey
* 1 cup sweet wine

Directions

Grate the apples on the coarse side of a box grater, sprinkling with lemon juice to prevent discoloring. In a large bowl add the other dry ingredients. Mix. Then add honey and sweet wine, and mix well. Cover and let marinate until Seder time.

Pink Sauce (for each cruet)

A favorite dressing for gefilte fish, hardboiled eggs, and artichokes.

Ingredients

* 1 cup virgin olive oil
* 1 tablespoon Gold's Red Horseradish
* 3 tablespoons finely chopped red onion
* 1 cup apple cider vinegar
* 1 tablespoon mayonnaise
* 2 ice cubes

Directions

Combine oil and vinegar. Add 1 tablespoon of red horseradish and 1 tablespoon of mayonnaise. Whip briskly; add more mayonnaise to get a nice pink color. Add chopped red onion. Add 2 ice cubes to keep mixture from separating.

Bob Kurtz

Bob Kurtz originally began in the Walt Disney story development department, then he animated on TV shows like *Roger Ramjet* before starting his own studio. He is known for Emmy and Peabody award-winning commercials like the Chevron "Dinosaur" and "Kitty Salmon." His feature work includes *City Slickers* (1991), *The Pink Panther* (2006), *Edith Ann Christmas*, and *Jurassic Park* (1993).

Inari Footballs by Bob Kurtz.

This is from Bob and his wife, Theresa Uchi Kurtz.

Footballs, a.k.a. Inari Sushi

The addition of pickled sushi ginger makes this version extra tasty.

Ingredients

* 2 2/5 cups short grain rice
* 2 2/5 cups water
* 3 tablespoons sake
* 3×2 inch piece konbu (dried kelp, also spelled kombu)
* 5 tablespoons vinegar (adjust to taste)
* 4 tablespoons sugar (adjust to taste)
* 2 teaspoons salt (add gradually to taste)
* 1/4 cup pickled sushi ginger (chopped)
* 1 teaspoon black sesame seeds (to taste)
* 1 package seasoned fried bean curd pouches (also known as ajistuke inari age)

Directions

Cook rice with water, sake, and konbu. After rice is cooked, let it set for 5 minutes. Pour the vinegar, sugar, and salt mixture over the rice and mix well, careful not to turn it into a glueball. Or skip this part and simply use the packet of powdered vinegar that comes with the fried bean curd! Add the pickled sushi ginger to the rice. Add sesame seeds if desired. Fill each bean curd pouch with rice.

Makes 12. Enjoy!

Pierre Lambert

Pierre Lambert is an animation historian, collector, and artistic consultant in France. His beautiful books of the art of Walt Disney's *Pinocchio*, *Bambi*, and *Sleeping Beauty* are prized throughout the world. This English translation was provided by his publisher, Dmitri Granovsky.

A favorite recipe…written at the end of a great summer.

Cep Smooth Veloute with Goose Foie Gras Balls

(**Note:** A cep [*boletus edulis*] is a category of edible mushroom found in Europe or North America. Porcini mushrooms are a good substitute.)

> Here is the recipe I love to cook for my friends: cep smooth velouté with goose foie gras (or without foie gras for vegetarians, but it's not so good!)

> **—Pierre Lambert**

Autumn has always been my favorite time of the year. Living in Normandy for more than 20 years, from mid-September to the end of October, I love leaving early in the morning to pick mushrooms in the company of my friend Philippe Guillemard, a talented and passionate cook. He introduced me to this ritual: do not get lost in the forest, carefully cut the feet of the mushrooms so that they can grow back, and, most importantly, know how to cook them!

This recipe is simple and delicious. Ceps can be replaced with, easier to find, cultivated mushrooms (we call them "champignons de Paris").

Directions

- Prepare small balls of raw foie gras and reserve them in the refrigerator. Little trick: cut a small dice of foie gras and roll it in the palm of your hand like plasticine.
- After carefully cleaning the ceps with a small knife (without washing), cut them into small quarters. Peel, wash, and finely chop the shallots.
- In a skillet, sweat the shallots in oil or butter over high heat for 2 minutes and add the ceps. Simmer covered for 10 minutes over low heat. Add 8.5 ounces of chicken broth and cook for another 5 minutes.
- Mix the preparation with the mixer, adding 2 tablespoons of cream, a pinch of salt, and pepper. Pour the hot soup in hot plates or small bowls and add the balls of foie gras. The heat of the velvety soup will lightly cook the outside of the greasy balls. It's an explosion of flavors in the mouth!

Good appetite, Madame, good appetite Monsieur!

- Oh, I forgot, a nice and lively Bourgeuil from the Loire Valley will add a delicate touch to this fine recipe...

PS: Before preparing this recipe, I recommend viewing *The Dance of the Mushrooms* from the *Nutcracker* sequence of *Fantasia*, masterfully cooked by Art Babbitt.

Robert Lence

Robert Lence cooking during a lecture series in Uruguay, 2013.

New York City born and bred, **Robert Lence** has been a storyboard artist, director, writer, and teacher in Hollywood for many years. His credits include *Toy Story, Beauty and the Beast, A Bug's Life*, and *Shrek*. An avid gourmet and former restaurant cook, he narrowly chose art school over chef's school.

Robert comes from a long line of "foodies." His grandmother used to make pasta for her entire town in Italy, and his mother Ann was a professional caterer. His grandparents would host elaborate dinners at the family homestead on Long Island, with delicacies that his grandfather had gathered from New York's Ninth Avenue and Little Italy.

Robert has cooked for his overseas animation colleagues on four continents, and loves to collect recipes wherever he lectures, be it Uruguay, China, Moscow, London, Mexico City, or Seoul.

This recipe, however, is one of his family favorites.

Manicotti. (Photo by Robert Lence.)

Manicotti

Crepes

Ingredients

* 1/2 cup whole milk
* 1/2 cup Wondra flour
* 2 eggs
* Pinch of salt
* Approximately 2 tablespoons butter

Directions

• Mix milk, flour, eggs, and salt in a blender until smooth. Let stand for 15 minutes.
• Butter a small 8-inch nonstick frying pan. Over medium heat, drop the batter into the pan with a 1/4-cup measuring cup. Swirl to cover the bottom of the pan completely. When the crepe is lightly browned on one side, flip it.
• Cook a few more minutes, until cooked through. Slide the crepe onto a plate to cool. Should make about 7 crepes.

Meat Sauce

Ingredients

* 1/3 cup extra-virgin olive oil
* 1/2 pound ground pork
* 1/2 pound ground beef (preferably chuck)
* 1/2 tablespoon ground fennel seed
* 1 tablespoon paprika
* 1 medium onion, chopped
* 2 garlic cloves, minced
* 1 (28-ounce) can whole peeled tomatoes (preferably San Marzano)
* 2 tablespoons tomato paste
* 1 (14.5 ounces) can of chicken stock
* 1/2 teaspoon salt, or to taste
* 1/4 teaspoon ground black pepper, or to taste
* 1/2 cup chopped fresh parsley

Directions

In a large pot or Dutch oven, heat the olive oil over medium heat. Add the meats, fennel, and paprika, and cook until lightly browned. Add the onion and garlic. Sautee until the meat is cooked through and the onion is soft. Add the canned tomatoes, tomato paste, chicken stock, salt, and pepper. Cook over medium-low heat for about 1½ hours.

Stir in the parsley.

Cheese Filling

Ingredients

* 15 ounces whole-milk ricotta cheese
* 1/2 pound mozzarella cheese, cubed
* 4 tablespoons grated Parmesan cheese

Direction

Combine the cheeses in a mixing bowl.

Topping

Ingredients

* 2 tablespoons grated Parmesan cheese
* 1/2 cup chopped fresh basil

Directions

- Preheat the oven to 400°F.

To assemble the Manicotti:

- In a 13 by 9-inch baking dish, spread the bottom of the dish with a layer of the meat sauce.
- Place some of the cheese mixture in a line in the center of each crepe, then fold over each end, into a tube shape. Arrange in the baking dish, seam side down. After all of the crepes are in the dish, top them evenly with the remaining meat sauce, making sure that all of the crepes are completely covered. (Note: If there is any extra sauce left over, you can heat it and serve it on the side.) Top with the remaining 2 tablespoons of grated Parmesan cheese.
- Bake for about 25 minutes, until bubbling.
- Top with the chopped fresh basil, and serve.
- Serves 4

Note: This recipe could easily be made vegetarian by eliminating the ground pork and beef, and substituting a can of vegetable stock for the chicken stock.

Bud Luckey

William "Bud" Luckey (1934–2018) was an animator, designer, and voice actor. From Billings, Montana, he served in the Air Force in the Korean War, and used his G.I. benefits to attend animation classes at Chouinard and USC. He became a protégé of Art Babbitt and began working with him at Quartet Films doing commercials. He later relocated to the San Francisco Bay Area where, among other clients, he formed a friendship with *Peanuts*-creator Charles Schulz, animating Charlie Brown for Dolly Madison cakes.

Bud is most well-known for his years at Pixar, joining the company early and, on *Toy Story*, creating the final design for the character Woody. He worked on *A Bugs Life, Finding Nemo, Ratatouille, Cars, WALL-E, Monsters Inc.,* and the *Toy Story* films.

Here is a recipe of Bud's from his son, Andy Luckey.

Bud's Spud Salad

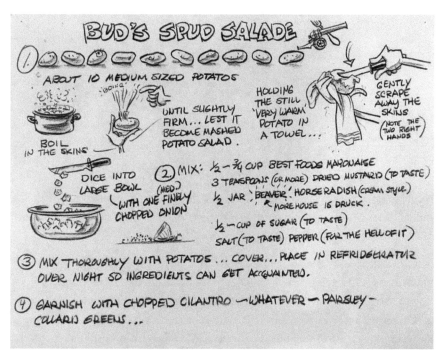

Buds Spuds by Bud Luckey. (Courtesy of Andy Luckey.) Note: When Bud writes "Morehouse is Druck," he meant to say "Morehouse is dreck" meaning not up to his standards.

Brice Mack and Ginni Mack

Ginni Mack. (Courtesy of Mindy Johnson.)

Brice Mack (1917–2003) was a story artist and background painter for Walt Disney. His credits include *Fantasia, Song of the South, Peter Pan,* and *Lady and the Tramp.* He later directed commercials and the live-action feature-film *Jennifer* (1978).

Ginni Mack worked at Walt Disney (see Ink & Paint Teatime), married Brice, and their son Kevin Mack won an Oscar for the visual effects on *What Dreams May Come* (1998). Ginni was a mainstay of the Disney Ink & Paint Department for many years and was the model for the design of Tinkerbell in *Peter Pan.* In 1990, when the traditional inks and paints were replaced by digital technology, Ginni was part of the first team to retrain as digital painters.

Yorkshire Pudding is not really pudding, as we would understand it. It is an Old English oven bread to be served alongside a meat and sauce dish, usually beef.

Ginni & Brice Mack's Yorkshire Pudding

Ingredients

* 1 cup flour
* 1 cup milk
* 1 cup water
* 1/2 teaspoon salt
* 2 eggs

Directions

Combine flour and salt. Mix milk and egg together—beat well, and add to dry ingredients. Beat well and add water. Let stand but beat at intervals. Pour into meat drippings and bake at 400°F for 1/2 hour. Serves 4 to 6 small servings.

Hayao Miyazaki

Hayao Miyazaki is considered one of the great animation directors of our time. His films *Spirited Away, My Neighbor Totoro*, and *Princess Mononoke* defined a golden age of Japanese anime, and in 2011, *Spirited Away* won an Academy Award.

When Miyazaki's animation crew is putting in all-nighters to complete a deadline, it is their custom to serve a meal for everyone around 11:00 p.m. The Ghibli Studio is equipped with a small kitchen and dining area. Even though they have that lounge area on their first floor, most of the team likes to eat at their desks and go back to work. The job of cooking rotates among the staff. Mr. Miyazaki himself has no problem cooking for the crew when his turn comes. Here is one of his recipes as interpreted by Robert Lence.

Poor Man's Salt Flavored Ramen "Aurora Style." (Photo by Robert Lence.)

Poor Man's Salt-Flavored Ramen, "Aurora Style"

Ingredients

* 4 cups vegetable stock (two 14.5-ounce cans)
* 6 cups water
* 5 packs instant ramen noodles with their seasoning packets (Dashi)
* 1 tablespoon miso
* 2 eggs (beaten)
* 1 cup of sliced mushrooms (shiitake, or enoki would do)
* 1/2 cup of sliced green onions
* Soy sauce
* Cooking oil

Directions

* In a large cooking pot, pour in the vegetable stock and the water and bring to a boil.
* Add the packs of ramen noodles and their accompanying seasoning mix and miso, and stir constantly.
* Slowly pour in the beaten eggs, while continuing to stir.
* Bring to a boil, then reduce heat and let simmer.
* Meanwhile, in a frying pan, heat cooking oil with a dash of soy sauce, and add in the mushrooms and green onions. Brown until tender.
* Mix the sautéed vegetables into the noodles and serve. Eat before the noodles get too soft.
* Serves 10

Tomm Moore

Tomm Moore. (Photo by Dylan Vaughn.)

Tomm Moore was born in Newry, Northern Ireland. Since starting Cartoon Saloon in Kilkenny Ireland with partners Nora Twomey and Paul Young, they've specialized in films styled with a particularly Celtic flavor. Ever since bursting onto the world scene in 2009 with Oscar-nominated *The Secret of Kells*, they have wracked up an impressive record. The Oscar-nominated *Song of the Sea* and *The Breadwinner* have both earned worldwide acclaim. Here is Tomm's vegan recipe:

Vegan Sweet Potatoes. (Courtesy of Tomm Moore.)

Vegan Sweet Potatoes

I have decided to go with my famous sweet potatoes.

It's a vegan recipe I've been whipping up for years now and was a favorite of my son's growing up.

It's pretty simple.

Ingredients

* Several large sweet potatoes
* Vegan margarine (2 tablespoons)
* Olive oil (3 tablespoons)
* Stem ginger preserved in syrup (usually it comes in jars); you need about two or three pieces chopped up
* Mixed spices (sometimes it's called allspice), about a tablespoon
* 2 crushed cloves of garlic
* Salt and cayenne pepper
* Thyme

Directions

* Start by cutting the sweet potatoes into 1/2-inch chunks and bake them until they are soft.
* Meanwhile sauté the garlic in vegan margarine and chop the ginger into small pieces.
* Add the soft sweet potatoes to the pan of sautéed garlic and ginger and add the syrup and olive oil.
* They will start to have a slightly blackened, candied crispy surface. Add the mixed spices and salt and pepper and serve! Add some thyme sprigs if you are feeling fancy!
* They go great with peas and some fried tofu or tempeh.

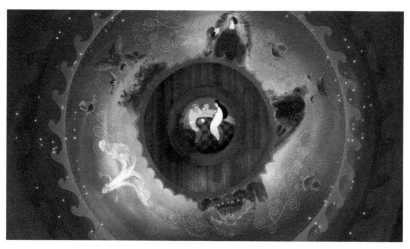

Tomm Moore Mural from *Song of the Sea*. (Courtesy of Tomm Moore.)

Myron Henry "Grim" Natwick

~

Grim Natwick by Richard Williams (1976). (Collection of the Author.)

Myron Henry "Grim" Natwick (1890–1990) was born in Wisconsin and studied drawing at the Ecole d'Beaux Arts in Paris. He became an animator at the Hearst Studio in 1918. He designed and animated the character Betty Boop for Max Fleischer in 1931. Later he went to Walt Disney to lead the team animating Snow White in Walt Disney's first feature film, *Snow White and the Seven Dwarfs*. He influenced a number of artists, who became the Nine Old Men, like Marc Davis, Ward Kimball, and Frank Thomas. He left Disney to return to Fleischer to animate Princess Glory in *Gulliver's Travels*, then later at UPA he created Nelly Bly for the John Hubley masterpiece *Rooty Toot Toot* (1951).

In 1973, he joined Richard William's team in London to help start the British animation resurgence. He animated on *The Adventures of Raggedy Ann & Andy* (1977) and *The Cobbler and the Thief*, where he continued to influence young, upcoming animators like Eric Goldberg and me.

Grim was known for his chili recipe. Here it is, as noted and interpreted by his longtime assistant and friend Dwayne Crowther.

Grim's Personal Chili

Grim's Chili. (Photo by Pat Sito.)

Ingredients

* 5 pounds burger meat (regular and extra lean combo)
* 4 large onions, coarsely chopped
* 4 bell peppers, coarsely chopped
* 6 large tomatoes, coarsely chopped
* 2 cloves garlic, minced

* 6 large cans kidney beans
* 2 small cans other beans (pinto or blackeye)
* 1 jar chili seasoning
* 1/2 jar cumin

Directions

* Fry burger meat with garlic, chili, and cumin. Reserve fat. Fry onions in fat.
* Put burger meat and onions in large pot with beans and peppers and tomatoes. Cook over low heat, stirring occasionally. Simmer couple of hours.

Optional

Ingredients

* 1 jar salsa fresca
* 1 large can stewed tomatoes
* Hot sauce

* 1 can pitted olives
* 1 can beer

Grim's drawing of Betty. (Collection of the Author.)

Grim Natwick lived to be 100 years old. For his centennial, the Hollywood animation community threw him a memorable banquet at the Sportsman's Lodge in Studio City (April 19, 1990). Over five hundred guests, from old legends Walter Lantz, Chuck Jones, Friz Freleng and Marc Davis, to newer computer pioneers like Chris Casady, attended. Grim Natwick died two months later. When Dwayne Crowther lamented his leaving, Grim smiled, "Well, what more do you want? TWO Hundred??"

Grim Natwick with friends on his 100th birthday, Aug. 1990. (Collection of the Author.)

Vip Partch

Virgil Partch (1916–1984), better known as "Vip" was born in Alaska. After graduating from Chouinard Art Institute, was hired as an animation assistant for the Walt Disney Studio. A supporter of the Animators Strike against Disney in 1941, he was soon on the street. He began submitting his gag cartoons to magazines, getting his first one printed in 1942. Vip Partch's distinctive style, evoking Ronald Searle with a UPA flair, was soon appearing in newspapers and magazines across the U.S. It was said when Pablo Picasso died in 1973, on his nightstand next to his bed, was a paperback book of Vip Partch cartoons.

Gag cartoon by Vip Partch. (Copyright of The Field Syndicate. Courtesy of the Cartoon Museum collection, San Francisco.)

Virgil Partch's Dinner Menu from the *Cartoonist's Cookbook*, 1966

- Swiss Canapé
- New England Clam Chowder
- Barbecued Herb Chicken
- Green Salad

- Fruit of the Season with Camembert Cheese
- Coffee
- Cigars
- Brandy
- Cigars
- Drambuie
- Cigars
- Double Brandy

Barbecued Herb Chicken

Ingredients

- 3 broiler chickens, halved
- 1/4 pound butter
- 1 tablespoon parsley, minced
- 1/2 teaspoon marjoram, minced
- 1/2 teaspoon tarragon, minced

- 1/2 cup salad oil
- 1 cup dry white wine
- 1/4 cup soy sauce
- 1 clove garlic, crushed
- 1/4 teaspoon salt

Directions

- Mix butter, parsley, tarragon, and marjoram. Using a dull knife, gently lift the skin from the breast of the halved chicken and insert the blend of butter and seasoning. Spread around under the skin as widely as possible, making sure the skin is not so detached as to come off when the chicken is turned on the grill.
- Make a marinade of the oil, wine, soy sauce, garlic, and salt. Let chicken stand in marinade overnight or, at least, for several hours, turning once during this period. Grill chicken, breast down, on a greased rack over glowing coals. Turn occasionally, basting with marinade, until golden brown—about 30 minutes. Serves 6.

Bill Plympton

New York–based **Bill Plympton** is one of the most well-known independent animators in the world today. Two-time Academy Award nominee, his distinctive style and wry sense of humor has graced dozens of short films and feature films, mostly drawn by himself. *Your Face* (1987), *Guard Dog* (2004), *Hair High* (2004), *The Tune* (1992), and *I Married a Strange Person* (1997).

Bill Plympton drawing. (Courtesy of Bill Plympton.)

Bill's Avocado Grapefruit Salad

So here is one of my favorite recipes: take 1 ripe avocado, dice it in a bowl, take a whole grapefruit - separate the slices and place in the bowl—add a couple of soup spoons of cottage cheese. I'd like to add a touch of mayonnaise (but that's me). Then if you want to get really extravagant, add some freshly peeled shrimp. It's one of my favorite meals, bon appetit!

Joanna Quinn

Joanna Quinn drawing. (Courtesy of Joanna Quinn.)

Joanna Quinn is an award-winning British independent animator. Her films include *Girls Night Out, Body Beautiful,* and *Dreams and Desires-Family Ties.*

Coq au Quinn

This is my take on coq au vin but I dare not call it by its proper French name because my French friends would be horrified! So here is my Quinn version. I cook it when the nights draw in and a bit of comfort food is needed. It also reminds me of my mum who was a wonderful cook and used to cook a fine coq au vin—but my mum's had more vin than coq!

Utensils

Heavy deep flame proof casserole dish—like le Creuset or similar.

Cooking Method

On the hob over gas/electric.

Ingredients

Ingredients (amounts based on what fits in my beloved medium-sized casserole dish).

* 6–8 filleted chicken thighs
* 4 large cloves of garlic
* Several glugs of olive oil
* 1 large or 2 medium red onion—medium to chunky slices
* 1 large red pepper—medium slices
* 1 stick of celery—medium slices
* 2 bay leaves
* 250 chestnut mushrooms—Most sliced and the rest chopped into 1/4s
* 1 bottle of full-bodied red wine
* Some sprigs of fresh rosemary and/or thyme
* 2 chicken stock pots[*] dissolved in 250 mls[†] of boiling water
* A healthy squirt of tomato puree
* An optional cheeky sprinkling of chili flakes or a 1/2 a chopped fresh chili if it's cold out (I can imagine French eye rolling and mutterings of "Mon Dieu" at this point.)

---

[*] Stock pots are available in the UK. Substitute chicken stock or bouillon cubes to create 250 ml of liquid.
[†] 250 ml = 8.4 ounces of liquid.

Directions

* Season the chicken with some salt and black pepper.
* Open the wine and pour yourself a glass.
* On a fairly high heat, put a large glug of olive oil into the casserole dish and brown the chicken in a couple of batches for about 6 minutes on each side. Once browned, put them onto a plate and to one side. Don't worry if the bottom of the casserole is a bit burnt looking; it all adds to the flavour later on. Turn down to a medium heat.
* Add the onions to the casserole and cook for about 5–10 mins until lightly coloured and soft, then add the celery, red pepper, and crushed garlic (and optional chili). Keep stirring so they don't burn. Once they are all soft, add the sliced mushrooms.

When the mushrooms are also soft, add the chicken pieces. Give it a good old stir then pour about a 1/2 of the bottle of wine into the casserole and add the tomato paste, stock, herbs, and bay leaves. Bring to boil and then lower the heat and put the lid on. Let it simmer away for about 30 mins, giving it the old stir to make sure it doesn't stick to the bottom. Also add a bit more of the wine if it needs more liquid.

- About 30 mins into cooking I take the lid off, and add the quartered mushrooms. From now on I put the lid 1/2 on, allowing for some of the liquid to evaporate and thicken. Cook for another 20 mins. At about 50 mins its probably ready to eat, but I like to take the lid off completely and keep it going for a wee bit longer just to make sure it's as rich as possible!
- At this point you go to pour yourself more wine but find it's all gone! Damn.
- Serve with green French beans and delicious Pembrokeshire (if in Wales) new potatoes or a big lump of fresh bread.

From *The Wife of Bath* by Joanna Quinn, 2011. (Courtesy of Joanna Quinn.)

George Scribner

George Scribner is an animation director-animator originally from Panama. George's credits includes *The Heavy Metal Movie* (1982), Ralph Bakshi's *American Pop* (1981), Walt Disney's *Oliver & Company* (1988), *Mickey's Prince and the Pauper* (1991), and *The Lion King* (1994).

From George and Debbie Scribner:

Panama Ceviche

Ingredients

* Any amount of seafood—Panamanians use corvina, which is white sea bass and inexpensive in Panama. You can also use shrimp, octopus, squid, or a mixture.
* Onion, chopped (one cup for every 3 cups seafood)
* About 1/2 cup red chopped red pepper (for color)
* Lime juice, enough to cover seafood completely
* Salt and pepper, to taste
* Hot sauce (picante) or jalapeño or habanero pepper, chopped (to taste)
* Chopped parsley
* Box of saltine crackers

Directions

* Chop fish into small, bite-sized pieces, and large shrimp into 3 or 4 pieces. Place in bowl.
* Add onion, red peppers, and hot sauce or hot pepper to taste.
* Cover everything in lime juice by at least 1/4 inch.
* Leave on kitchen counter, two hours for shrimp, 6 to 8 hours for fish (fish will turn white).*
* After "cooking" in lime juice, if the seafood is too watery, pour out some of the juice.
* Refrigerate until cold. Will keep for 3 to 4 days.
* Serve with topping of parsley and saltine crackers. Enjoy with rum & coke or beer!

---

*Some may not like the idea of leaving the fish out to marinate in the lime juice. Putting in the fridge is alright too, although it may take longer to "cook."

Tom Sito

Born in New York City, **Tom Sito** moved out to Hollywood and was an animator and story artist for many years. His credits include *Who Framed Roger Rabbit* (1988), *Beauty and the Beast* (1991), *The Lion King* (1994), *Shrek*, and *Osmosis Jones* (2001), and also TV series like *He-Man and the Masters of the Universe* (1983), and *She-Ra, The Princess of Power* (1985). When not drawing, Sito had a lifelong obsession with history, which inspired him to become the author of a number of books on animation history, including this one.

"One of my favorite dishes to make for friends is a two thousand year old recipe from ancient Rome. It first appeared in Marcus Gavius Apicius, *De re Coquinaria, On the Subject of Cooking*. Written in the first century AD, it is one of the world's oldest cookbooks (only some Babylonian clay tablets from 1,700 BCE are older). While some Roman dishes like stuffed dormice, peacock brains, or whole roast flamingo don't quite appeal to a modern palate anymore, other Roman dishes can prove quite tasty. This one is for pork roast in apricot gravy.

Roman dinner by Tom Sito.

Roman Pork Roast

Ingredients

- 3½ pound pork loin or pork shoulder roast
- A dozen sweet, ripe apricots, stoned and halved (A can of apricot halves drained will work too.)
- 2 tablespoons of olive oil
- Shallots
- Dry red wine
- Wine vinegar
- Sherry or Malaga wine
- 1/2 teaspoon of peppercorns
- Ground pepper
- Honey (Romans loved honey. Europeans had not discovered sugar yet.)
- Dill weed, dried mint, cumin seed
- Biscuit or shortbread crumbs

Liquamen, or **Garum**, was an all-purpose condiment that the Romans put on everything, much like our ketchup. And like ketchup, because it was so ubiquitous, the Romans didn't bother to explain what it was made of, so the recipe is lost to history. You can experiment with the Vietnamese fish sauce nuoc nam, but to save yourself a lot of trouble, I just use soy sauce.

Directions

- Set your oven for 375°F.
- Roast the pork on a rack for 1 hour and 45 minutes. When done, remove the pork and cut it up into cubes, trimming off the fat. Collect the fat and drippings and set aside.
- Heat 3 tablespoons of olive oil in a large skillet. Add 2 tablespoons (a fistful) of chopped shallots and cook for 2 minutes. Add 2 teaspoons of liquamen (soy sauce), and a cup of dry red wine. Bring to a boil, then reduce the heat. Stir in the diced pork, cover and let simmer for 15 minutes.
- In another small saucepan, add a teaspoon each of ground cumin seed, dill weed, and dried mint, plus a tablespoon of honey, a 1/4 cup of Malaga or Sherry, the pork dripping, a teaspoon of wine vinegar, and another splash of soy sauce (liquamen).
- After it gets going, add a 1/2 cup of the liquid the pork has been simmering in.
- Bring to a boil. Add the apricots and simmer for 10 minutes. Stir in the biscuit crumbs to thicken the mixture slightly.
- Separate the pork cubes from the liquid in the pan and place in a serving bowl. Pour the sauce over the pork and garnish with freshly ground pepper.
- I serve it over rice or noodles, even though noodles aren't exactly Roman. For a side dish, you can sauté sliced carrots in olive oil, honey, and a pinch of cumin. Serve with hummus, flatbread, olives, and grapes of course. To be really Roman, you don't use forks, as they were not invented yet. A tablespoon, flatbread, and your fingers are best.
- Wrap yourself in a bed sheet as a toga, lie out on a couch, and enjoy! An orgy later is optional.

Genndy Tartakowsky

Genndy Tartakowsky was born in Russia when it was the Soviet Union. His family moved to America when he was seven. After graduating Cal Arts, he went into animation. He is the creator of the series *Dexter's Laboratory, Samurai Jack* and *Star Wars: The Clone Wars.* He also directed the *Hotel Transylvania* trilogy and *The Powerpuff Girls Movie.*

From Genndy:

Katleti: Soviet Union Comfort Food

The word Soviet Union and comfort usually don't belong together, but the Russian people are a strong bunch and knew how to handle oppression: Eat a lot and Drink a lot!

My mom was a great cook, her mom was a great cook, and I'm sure since the first days of our family they were all good cooks. I came out of the womb overweight and well fed, and no matter what happens in my life, I turn to the food my mom made in times of stress and discomfort. One dish in particular that was my favorite and I have continued on making for my family…KATLETI.

Basically, almost every culture has a version of this food, it's a ground chicken patty/burger type of thing. Whenever I feel sad, nostalgic, stressed, or on a grey cloudy day, it's good soul food.

Ingredients

(This serves about a family of 6, or a Russian family of four.)

* 3 pounds ground chicken thighs
* 1 loaf of white bread (any old bread will do though)
* 3/4 onion
* Olive oil
* 1 tablespoon butter
* 1 egg
* 1/2 tablespoon crushed red pepper
* Dill
* Salt and pepper to taste

Directions

- Start with the loaf of bread. I prefer a good Italian round or French bread; this will be our breadcrumbs. If you want to try it old school, you can take some old stale bread and soak it in milk, squeeze the moisture out, and then grind it with the chicken for best results. Roughly cut up the bread into 1-inch squares, and bake in the oven for about 45 minutes or until it is completely moisture-free but not burned. Throw the bread into a food processor (with some salt and pepper) and grind it fine. Then chop up your onion very fine; this is somewhat of a pet peeve of mine as some of the other moms in our neighborhood would barely chop up the onion and it would taste more like an onion burger. Saute the onions in the butter until nice and golden or even a little brown. Combine the chicken, about half the breadcrumbs, egg, crushed red pepper, salt and pepper, and onions. Mix it all together well, but not overly mixed, and make patties; wet your hands to make it more manageable. My wife and daughters like their's breaded; that's not traditional, but they love the taste.
- Heat up some olive oil that goes about an 1/8 inch up in a 12-inch pan or so and start frying up in batches. Cook until each side is golden brown. Be patient, use a low–medium flame and only turn once. Garnish with dill and you're ready to go. It needs a potato side dish so I recommend a creamy buttery mash or slowly sautéed with some onions (finely chopped) in oil and butter.

Don Tobin

Don Tobin (1916–1995) was from Austin Texas. After graduating from Berkeley in 1936, his drawing talent landed him a job at the Walt Disney Studio. He is credited as an animator on *Pinocchio, Bambi, Dumbo, Fantasia, The Nifty Nineties,* and *The Reluctant Dragon.*

He was a supporter of the 1941 Disney animators strike. After leaving the studio, and a stint in the service in WWII, he went to New York to become a top cartoonist for *The New Yorker* magazine. His feature was called *The Little Woman.* His work also appeared in Colliers and the Saturday Evening Post.

This is a reprint of one of his preferred dishes from the National Cartoonist Council's *The Cartoonists Cookbook* (1966).

Fondue Bourguignonne—Don Tobin

Ingredients

* Beef filet or good quality sirloin cut into 1-inch cubes, allowing 1/2 pound or more per person
* 1/4 pound butter
* 2 cups peanut oil

Directions

Heat oil and butter in a fondue pot over range burner until hot, then transfer pot to alcohol burner on dining table. Oil must be quite hot, but not boiling, to make this dish a success. Meat is cooked by spearing with wooden-handled forks or skewers and immersing in hot oil for a few minutes until it reaches desired degree of doneness. Meat is then dipped into one of a variety of sauces and eaten. (To avoid burnt lips, for Heaven's sake, use regular fork for eating.)

The number of sauces used is limited only by one's imagination. Some that we have found good are the following:

- Béarnaise sauce
- Remoulade
- Mayonnaise with curry powder
- Russian dressing
- Chili sauce
- Mustard sauce

This is all apt to be a bit rich, so along with the sauces it's a good idea to have a wide variety of side dishes such as:

- Chopped onions
- Capers
- Mushrooms
- Olives
- Radishes
- Cucumbers marinated in Italian dressing
- Grated carrots in mayonnaise
- Celery
- Tossed green salad

The more your plate is loaded with a variety of tastes, the more fun the dish. Serve with lots of French bread and a red wine.

Marshall Toomey

Marshall J. Toomey began his career on the film *Heavy Metal* (1983), then Don Bluth's *The Secret of Nimh*. Moving on to Walt Disney, he became a mainstay of the assistant animation department. His talents were essential to films like *Beauty and the Beast, Mulan, Tarzan, Princess and the Frog*, and *The Lion King*.

Marshall is caricatured in *Aladdin* as one of the street vendors Aladdin upsets in his opening song "One Step."

Marshall loves to cook and brought the flavors of his hometown to our cartoon community in Burbank.

Pesto-Butter Salmon

Ingredients

* 2 pounds salmon with skin
* Salt and pepper
* Asparagus, cleaned
* 1 yellow squash, sliced
* 3 tablespoons pesto
* 3 tablespoons butter
* 3 tablespoons white wine

Directions

Mix pesto and butter together in a small bowl. Place salmon, skin side down in a medium-heated pan. Cook 5–7 minutes. Add yellow squash and asparagus around the sides of the pan. Add wine. Place lid on the pan. Cook on medium heat until desired doneness or about 10 minutes.

Yummmmmmmm!

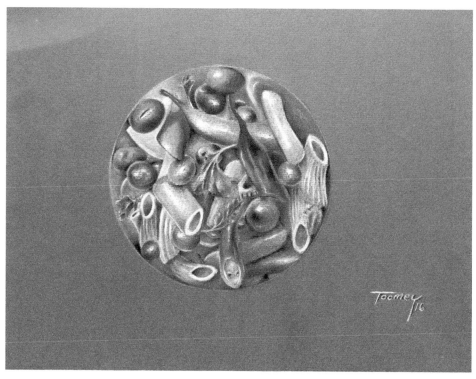

Drawing by Marshal Toomey. (Courtesy of Marshall Toomey.)

Ben Washam

Ben Washam. (Photo courtesy of Jean Washam.)

Ben Washam (1915–1984) was born in Arkansas and moved to Los Angeles fairly early in his life. He was one of the key animators on the Chuck Jones unit during all his great Warner Bros. short cartoons. Chuck usually entrusted Ben with the final closeup of Bugs looking into camera and saying something pithy: "… And mud, spelled backwards, is dumb." Ben followed Chuck out of Warner Bros. in 1963 to animate *Tom & Jerry* shorts for MGM, and then Chuck's famous TV specials, like *The Grinch Who Stole Christmas*. Ben was president of the Screen Cartoonists Guild for two terms. In his final active years, he would give animation instruction to young wannabe animators out of his garage in Laurel Canyon. All the young trainees at Hanna-Barbera knew about Tuesday nights at Bennie's Class. He did it all for free. I once asked him why he did not charge people, or work through a school. He said animation had been very good to him, and this was his way of paying it back.

Ben also had an interesting side-life. During the Great Depression, before he was hired at an animation studio, he got a job at a Glendale restaurant called The White Log Tavern. He developed into a pretty good cook. Like a fry-cook, he was ever sporting a toothpick in the corner of his mouth, and his tummy looked natural with an apron wrapped around it. Around 1936, he became friends with another cook named Bob Wian. Bob would tell him "Bennie, why don't ya quit this cartoon business? I got plans for a big restaurant, and we can be partners!" Ben preferred to stay in animation, but as a favor to his friend, he designed his restaurants logo—Bob's Big Boy.

Thanks to Jean Washam, here is one of Bennie's favorite dishes.

Orange-Stuffed Porkchops

Ingredients

* 2 cups dry breadcrumbs
* 1/2 teaspoon nutmeg
* 1/2 cup cut up prunes
* 1 cup diced orange pulp
* 6 1-inch pork chops with pockets
* 2 tablespoons of lard or drippings
* 1½ teaspoons of salt
* 1/8 teaspoon of pepper
* 1/4 cup of orange juice
* 1/4 cup of water

Directions

* Combine the breadcrumbs, nutmeg, prunes, and orange pulp. Stuff the pork chops with this mixture. Brown the chops in lard or drippings. Pour off excess drippings. Season chops with salt and pepper. Add orange juice and water.
* Cover tightly and let simmer 45 minutes to 1 hour, or until tender.
* Makes 6 servings.

Fried Zucchini Sticks

Slice zucchini lengthwise. Whip two eggs in a bowl. Dip zucchini in egg, coat with cracker crumbs. Then, fry until golden brown and crisp on both sides.

Gag drawing of Ben leaving Warner Bros. for UPA. (Courtesy of Jean Washam.)

Alex Williams

Alex Williams is an English animator and son of famed animator **Richard Williams**. He went to college originally to study law and became a barrister in London. While working as a research assistant at the House of Commons, Alex created a comic strip that ran in the London Times called *The Queens Counsel*. For this strip he was awarded the Cartoon Art Trust Award for Strip Cartooning in October 2017. He has animated on films like *The Iron Giant, Who Framed Roger Rabbit, Monster House, Spirit Stallion of the Cimarron,* and *Open Season*.

Poisson a la BAFTA*

Ingredients

* Fish
* Potatoes
* Stock
* Spring onions

* Peas
* Other nice veg
* Some cooked prawns

---

*British Academy of Film and Television Arts

Directions

- Dust the fish in flour and seasoning.
- Chop your veg into little pieces.

Cooking

- Boil the potatoes and mash them. Stir in lots of yummy flavours like mustard, soy sauce, and big handfuls of chopped herbs.
- Fry up the veg—whatever you have. Add garlic, spring onions. Boil some peas lightly. Put the veg to one side and keep warm.
- Make some gravy by making some stock (not too much—it can be very salty), add a little flour to thicken, and then adding this to the frying pan that the veg was in. Flavor it with whatever you have such as soy sauce, Worcester sauce, white wine, sherry. Yum—make lots.
- Get the pan really hot and add a generous amount of butter. Just before the butter starts to burn, add the fish, skin side down so it sizzles. Turn the fish over and cook on both sides. The idea is to get the skin really crispy. Don't overcook.
- Put the mash in shallow soup plates and pop the fish on top of it. Add the veg around the edges of the mash and pour in the gravy so it makes a moat. Garnish with prawns.

Comic Strip by Alex Williams. (Courtesy of Alex Williams.)

Enid Denbo-Wizig

Enid Denbo Wizig progressed from the Walt Disney Ink & Paint Department into Animation in the 1940s. Enid trained with Art Babbitt, Bill Melendez, and Chuck Jones at the Schlesinger Studios and animated on *Bugs Bunny* and many of the *Merrie Melodies* cartoons.

This tasty recipe for cheese blintzes was a favorite family recipe, which her mother handed down to Enid!

Cheese Blintzes

Filling

Ingredients

* 1/2 pound hoop cheese

  (If you can't find hoop cheese, use whole, part skim, or non-fat ricotta cheese, fully drained.)
* 1/2 pound farmer's cheese
* Juice from half of a small lemon (approx—to taste)
* 1 teaspoon cinnamon (approx—to taste)
* 4 teaspoons granulated sugar (approx—to taste)
* 1 teaspoon sour cream (approx—to taste)
* 2 eggs
* Pinch salt
* 1 teaspoon plain breadcrumbs or cracker meal

Crepe

Ingredients

* 3 eggs
* 1 cup all purpose flour, sifted
* 1 cup cold milk
* 1 teaspoon sugar
* 1/2 cup water
* Butter for the pan

Directions

- In a medium bowl, mix together the two types of cheese. If you are using hoop cheese, you will need to press the cheese through a large mesh strainer so it will be easier to blend. Add in the lemon juice, cinnamon, sugar, and sour cream, adding more if preferred. Beat the two eggs, add a pinch of salt, and add the beaten eggs to the cheese. Add the breadcrumbs or cracker meal. Set aside the cheese mixture.
- To make the crepe batter, first beat the eggs in a medium bowl. Slowly add the sifted flour and mix to form a paste. Add the milk, a little at a time, keeping the paste smooth. Slowly add the sugar and the water. Pour the batter through a fine mesh sieve to remove any lumps that may have formed. To cook the crepes, melt a small amount of butter to cover the bottom of a 6- or 8-inch nonstick crepe pan. Once the butter is melted, pour enough batter to cover the bottom when you tilt the pan to spread it around (not too thick). Cook the crepe until the edge is slightly brown. When the crepe is cooked, flip the pan upside down over a clean dish towel that you've laid out on the counter. Repeat. Allow the crepes to cool on the towel and do not stack.
- Once the crepes are cooled, place about a tablespoon of the cheese mixture into the center of the crepe. Fold the bottom of the crepe over the filling, then the top of the crepe over the filling, then fold over both sides of the crepe until the cheese mixture is fully covered and the blintz forms a small rectangle. Fry each blintz in butter until lightly browned on both sides. Serve warm with sour cream and jam.

Practical Jokes

Drawing by Walt Kelly of animators Ward Kimball and Fred Moore as prize fighters. Bill Tytla is the referee, and Walt Kelly the time-keeper. (Circa 1940.) (Collection of the Author.)

One thing studio animators did while working hard, was occasionally to play hard. During the years of drawing and painting restricted to a chair within a close office space, horseplay was common. Over the open cubicle spaces, wadded up paper-ball barrages occasionally lightened the mood. Long rubber bands used to wrap scene folders were commandeered for use in some pretty intense paper-clip fights. Famed animation director Tex Avery lost sight in one eye because of a direct hit from a paper clip (or it may have been a pushpin) in such a fight. Max Fleischer animators folded a paper airplane large enough for four men to carry and launched it out their 9th floor window down onto Broadway. 35 mm metal film can lids from editorial stood in for Frisbee catch. Even decades later, animators recalled fondly some of the more celebrated practical jokes their comrades perpetrated on each other.

In the Schlesinger Studio, the early 1930s soda-pop machine was a large, horizontal refrigerator tank of cold water, with the bottles of Coca Cola held in the water by mechanical claws. Depositing a quarter released a bottle to you. One time Tex Avery snuck over to the cooler and emptied some of the Coke bottles, refilling them with 86 proof Scotch. He refitted the caps, then placed them back into the water as though nothing was unusual. You can imagine the surprise of the unsuspecting co-worker expecting to refresh his palate with Coke, only to find out he was pouring Johnny Walker down his throat!

Voice actor Matt Hurwitz recalled meeting Tex Avery at the Nuart Theater during a retrospective of his work. Tex said, "Guys would always be messin'" around—shooting spitballs, or crawling under another guy's desk and putting a match in his shoe and lighting it. "We went, "Wait a minute—a HOTFOOT?? You guys actually did that???" He said, "Oh, yeah—ruined a fella's shoes and everything."

One animator on Bob Clampett's unit liked to keep a can of beer on his desk that he'd take an occasional swig from while he was drawing. Once, while he was away from his desk, another artist emptied the can of beer and replaced it with his own urine. The returned artist was about to take a drink when the others lost their nerve and stopped him just in time!

Another time, Looney Tunes animator Ben Washam emptied an entire water cooler bottle and refilled it with his own personal Bloody Mary mixture.

Ben Washam once ordered a delivery of a pitcher of martinis from the local bar, sealed in a tin canister. To allay suspicion, he instructed the courier to meet him at the bottom of the back stairs. He had just paid the man, when who should be walking over to him but studio boss Leon Schlesinger! Ben thought his goose was cooked! Then Leon casually mentioned to him that his getting deliveries like this looked suspicious and might cause talk. Next time, he should have all his orders sent to the front entrance!

One Disney animator once put a dead fish inside the light box of his unsuspecting neighbor. Another time, a cake of Limburger cheese. Time, and the heat from the table's light bulbs, soon made the smells unbearable.

Disney assistant Stan Green said Nine Old Men master animator Marc Davis liked to position his desk so he could look up from his work to see who was entering his room. The floor in the hallways was all linoleum, so you could hear footsteps coming to your door. Stan and fellow assistant Bud Hester would creep up to either side of Marc's door. Bud would walk loudly up to the doorway but stop just short of coming into view, Then Stan would resume the footsteps from the others side walking away. They knew Marc would be watching. They kept this up until they drove Marc crazy with distraction!

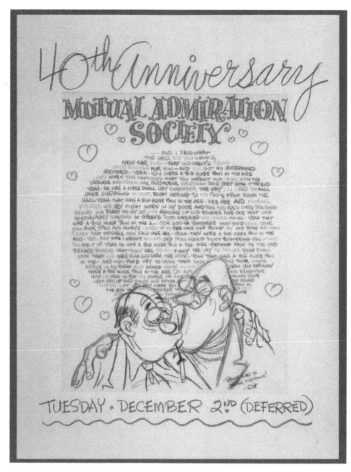

The Milt Kahl, Mark Davis 40th Anniversary. (Courtesy of Alice Davis.)

On Disney's *Sleeping Beauty*, assistant Iwao Takamoto was the key cleanup artist of Prince Phillip. He reviewed all the in-betweeners drawings to make sure they remained consistently on model. Any incorrect line Iwao would erase and draw in correctly in red. At the end of the week there would be a line of artists with their in-betweens, waiting to have them reviewed by Iwao. Fellow lead key cleanup artist Stan Green once took a young in-betweeners drawings and sprayed acrylic fixative on them. When it got to Iwao, and he began attempting to erase incorrect lines, they wouldn't erase! Iwao went crazy trying to erase them before he realized he had been the subject of a prank.

Iwao himself also contributed to the pranks. A small man, one day after lunch Iwao climbed inside Milt Kahl's large desk and hid. Milt soon came back to his desk and proceeded to begin drawing. Iwao waiting until Milt was deep in concentration, "The Zone," when he suddenly grabbed both his ankles! Milt let out a loud scream, jumped up, and let loose with a torrent of Anglo-Saxon expletives for which he was famous for. Iwao later went on to become famous as a designer at Hanna & Barbera, creating characters like Scooby Doo.

Animation director Jack Kinney recalled Walt Disney had a habit of walking into your office without knocking. He figured he owned everything anyway, why stand on formality? One day in 1936 he was showing around VIPs Charlie Chaplin and H. G. Wells, while explaining the animation process. As he walked up to the door of composers Frank Churchill and Paul Smith, Walt explained "And here's the room where the boys are composing the music for Snow White …." He opened the door to see the two men bent over a piano lighting each other's farts.

The Baking of Greyskull by Tom Sito. (Collection of the Author).

Animator Ken Muse had an extraordinary career at MGM animating *Tom & Jerry*. By the late 1970s, work and hard living had aged him prematurely. He hobbled around Hanna-Barbera with the aid of two canes. One day while Ken was working intently, one wag took his two canes, removed the rubber tips, sawed an inch off and replaced the tips. A day later, they sawed off another inch. And so on, until poor Ken was walking practically doubled over.

At the Filmation Studios in the 1980s, we had a large Ink & Paint department. Many of them were middle aged and older women, veterans of many years of service in various studios' paint departments. Their office was assigned a quiet production assistant named Julio who did much of the menial tasks to keep the painters supplies in stock. One year, on his birthday, the ladies thought it would be fun to get him a strip-o-gram birthday greeting. These strippers would usually gain entrance to a facility by disguising themselves in some kind of uniform. This time a pretty blonde woman came to Julio dressed as an immigration officer come to arrest him! What everybody did not know was first off Julio was gay, so the beautiful ingénue did not interest him, and he really was working in the U.S. illegally. Even when the stripper was straddling him wearing nothing but a black lace thong, instead of being excited, Julio looked terrified! Years later I heard he earned his U.S. citizenship and became a successful businessman.

Another time a rather tall, burly man dressed in work clothes with a tool belt, came through the department. He looked like the lumberjack on the cover of Brawny-brand paper towel packages. A small knot of painters clustered around him. "Why are you here?" They asked. "I'm here to inspect the fire extinguishers." was his reply. The ladies were dubious. "Come on. That's not a real job. Who are you REALLY here for?"

Turned out he really was a fire extinguisher inspector! Yet as he walked through the halls, a crowd of matronly ladies followed him with comments like "Hurry up and get your pants off! Lets see what you got, beefcake. Where's your boombox?" The poor man fled absolutely mortified.

Sometimes old college rivalries inspired the horseplay. On the Walt Disney production *Pocahontas*, we had two associate producers, one a graduate of USC and the other a graduate of UCLA. The two were always bombing each others' offices. The USC gal would open her office in the morning to find herself waist deep in baby-blue and gold balloons and white teddy Bruin stuffed bears. Another time the UCLA guy found his desk festooned with cardinal and gold ribbons and Tommy-Trojan dolls.

Even though the days of pencils, brushes, and paints have given way to digital paint and compositing, as long as you have large offices of artists committing pranks to pass the time and amuse one another, this tradition will go on.

Gag drawing by Thom Enriquez about my leaving Walt Disney's *Dinosaur* project to go to DreamWorks, 1995.

Baked Dishes and Desserts

Clarence "Ducky" Nash and friend eating ice cream. (Collection of the Author.)

Ink & Paint Teatime

TEA-TIME

"Teatiming" by Rae Medby McSpadden. (Courtesy of the McSpadden Family.)

From Mindy Johnson: For decades, the stronghold for women artists in animation could be found within the various Ink & Paint departments. These women were artists in their own right, but their artistry and contributions to the end results of animation were often overlooked.

Late in the 1920s, Walt Disney recognized the sedentary context of the work these women accomplished for each animated film and instituted a regular 15-minute "tea break" for the ladies, twice a day. Providing a chance to break-up the day, "teatiming" gave the ladies a chance to move about, stretch, and rest their eyes—necessary resets considering the long hours and painstaking work their roles required.

At the Hyperion Studio in the 1930s, a uniformed maid set up large tables at the back of the Ink & Paint rooms and lined each with china teacups and saucers. She would announce each break by ringing a bell and calling 'teatime' promptly at 10 am and 3 pm. Legendary Ink & Paint artist Ruthie Tompson puzzled at the addition of coffee during "teatime." She recalled the response: "Well, the Inkers have to have tea because coffee makes them have the shakes." Painters could have coffee.

On Fridays, Lorna Doone shortbread cookies were served and when in season, Mallomar cookies were a special treat for the Ink & Paint forces. During the hot summer days, "George" the Good Humor ice cream man, roamed the hallways of the Hyperion Studios. As the studio newsletter reported, George kept "an intricate credit system" for those who may not have had the five cents and "acted as a sort of frozen cupid by delivering prepaid sundries to surprised Secretaries and Inkers and Painters."

In 1940, when the Disney Studios began production at their Burbank Studio location, the Walt Disney Ink & Paint Department was renowned for its quality. With its state-of-the-art color lab and the finest materials at their disposal to achieve the height of animation artistry with ink-pens and paintbrushes, Disney's was known as "The Country Club." Gatherings and celebrations continued within Ink & Paint where tradition held that each artist brought in a sharable treat for everyone on their birthday. Many delectable treats and savory dishes were enjoyed between the long hours of production.

The welcomed oasis for the feminine forces was the Tea Room featuring a secluded sun deck speckled with shaded resort chairs where the ladies could "loosen their blouses" and so enjoy a bit of sunbathing. For decades, a lively and spirited British woman named Vera LeLean ran the Tea Room strictly according to protocol, including proper Tea Cakes ordered from a local Burbank establishment named Martino's Bakery, which is still in operation.* While their renowned teacake recipe is top secret, these small square treats were a standard part of everyday operations at the Disney Ink & Paint Tea Room for nearly 50 years.

Ink & Paint Department, 1987. (Collection of the Author.)

---

* In August 1990, when the animation industry legends gathered to celebrate the 100th Birthday of Betty Boop creator Grim Natwick, he requested that his birthday cake be made by Martinos.

"Lorna-Doones" Shortbread Cookies

Far from sugar cookies, shortbread cookies are meant to be a bridge between cream and fruit and are generally served with ice cream.

Ingredients

* 2 sticks salted butter—plus 2 tablespoons softened butter
* 1 cup sugar
* 2 cups all-purpose flour
* 1 cup (approximately) cornstarch

Directions

- Add 2 sticks of butter along with 2 tablespoons softened butter with sugar and beat together until fluffy.
- Sift flour and just under a cup of cornstarch together into a bowl. With a pastry cutter, incorporate the flour mixture into the butter/sugar mixture. If too crumbly, cut in up to 1 tablespoon of salted butter, as needed. Form into a ball and wrap in plastic wrap or Ziploc bag—refrigerate for 20 minutes.
- Preheat oven to 325°F. Lightly flour your baking surface and rollout dough to 1/4 to 1/3-inch thick. With preferred round biscuit or cookie cutter, cut cookies and place on cookie sheet with parchment paper and bake for 20 minutes (at 325°F). These should evenly have the slightest golden tinge—do not let the shortbread brown. Let the cookies cool slightly on the cookie sheet before removing them to finally cool.

Simple Mallomar Cookies

Graham Cracker Base

Ingredients

* 10 ounces crushed graham cracker crumbs
* 1 1/2 sticks (6 ounces) unsalted butter, melted

Directions

Base preparation—in a large bowl, mix graham cracker crumbs and butter until even and firmly press mixture into the bottom of 9 × 13" pan. Set aside.

Marshmallow Middle

Ingredients

* 4 teaspoons gelatin
* 1/2 cup water (divided)
* 1/2 cup light corn syrup (divided)
* 1 cup and 2 tablespoons (approximately 9 ounces) granulated sugar
* 1 teaspoon pure vanilla extract

Directions

- In a small bowl, place 1/4 cup of water and sprinkle gelatin over the top. Let sit at least 5 minutes to soften.
- Place 1/4 cup corn syrup in mixer bowl. Stir remaining 1/4 cup corn syrup, remaining 1/4 cup water, and sugar in medium saucepan over medium-high

heat until dissolved. Cook—without stirring—until mixture reaches 240°F on a thermometer.

- Immediately pour hot syrup into mixing bowl and add the softened gelatin and vanilla. Mix at medium speed until ingredients are combined (approximately 1 minute), then increase the speed to medium high until the mixture is light and fluffy (approximately 8 minutes) Pour marshmallow mixture over the graham cracker based and smooth with a spatula. Chill for approximately 30 minutes or until set.

Chocolate Topping

Ingredients

- ❊ 4 ounces bittersweet chocolate—finely chopped
- ❊ 1/2 cup heavy cream

Directions

- Place chopped chocolate pieces in a medium bowl. In a small saucepan, heat cream until simmering and pour over chocolate—whisk briskly until melted and smooth. Pour over set marshmallow layer and chill until chocolate is set (approximately 15 minutes).
- Cut into vertical and horizontal rows to create approximately 24 squares and serve!

Ink & Paint Tearoom Tea Cakes

Yields 24 teacakes.

Teacake

Ingredients

* 1 1/4 cups brown sugar
* 3/4 cup extra fine white sugar
* 3/4 cup vegetable oil
* 3/4 teaspoon salt
* 1/2 teaspoon vanilla

* 3 eggs
* 1 1/2 cups buttermilk
* 2 1/2 cups cake flour
* 1/2 teaspoon baking soda

Directions

* In mixing bowl, cream brown sugar, white sugar, vegetable oil, salt, and vanilla. Fold in eggs and cream slowly for 6 minutes, carefully scraping down the bowl sides. Add 3/4 cup of the buttermilk, cake flour, and baking soda. Mix until smooth. Add the remaining 3/4 cup of buttermilk and thoroughly mix. Batter will have a thin consistency.
* Line a square muffin pan with round paper liners. Fill cups approximately 2/3 full and bake at 375°F for 18–20 minutes. Cool in pan for 5–10 minutes, then remove to cooling rack. Let completely cool before adding glaze.

Glaze

Ingredients

* 6 tablespoons butter
* 1 1/2 cups powdered sugar

* 1 teaspoon vanilla
* 3 tablespoons hot water

Directions

- Melt butter completely (microwave—approximately 1 minute). Frequently stir while melting—do not overheat the butter. In a separate bowl, mix powdered sugar, vanilla, and hot water together to form a paste. Add the melted butter and whisk until smooth.
- While the glaze is still warm (and the cakes are completely cooled), dip the tops of each teacake into the glaze and set aside to cool (until the glaze hardens). If glaze is too thin, add a bit more powdered sugar.

Disney Ink & Paint Artists on TeaBreak. (Courtesy of Alan Coates.)

Ink & Paint Party Treats

With various generations of women working together, there were frequent gatherings and celebrations throughout the ranks of Ink & Paint. News of engagements, weddings, showers, retirements, and the completion of various films always prompted potlucks, buffets, and smorgasbords spread out on the Paint Department order desk.

Holidays also marked a prime time for parties with accompanying treats prevalent throughout the Ink & Paint Department. Hat Day, Tacky Day, Hawaiian Day were just a few of the various celebrations beyond the seasonal highlights of Halloween and the Christmas Holidays. In the 1970s, hungry young animators sought invites to the Ink & Paint parties since they served the best food! Here are just a few examples of favorites served among the Disney Ink & Paint ranks:

Ink & Paint artists on *The Great Mouse Detective* throwing a retirement party. Tanya Moreau Smith (red hair), Saskia Raevouri (far right). (Courtesy of Tina Price.)

Janet Bruce

Janet Bruce held a 40-year career in animation as a Painter, Xerox Processor, Color Model Supervisor and Animation Check Supervisor. Janet was one of the early artists to transition at the forefront of the digital age with the Disney CAPS system in the early 1990s.

In the 1980s, Janet copied this recipe from a magazine while waiting in a dentist's office, but forgot to copy the title. Her family loved the bars, and immediately dubbed them "Fat Bars." These "sinfully delicious" bars were a regular favorite at the legendary Disney Ink & Paint potluck gatherings.

Fat Bars

Ingredients

Blend together and mix well:

* 1 1/2 cups graham cracker crumbs
* 1 can Borden's Sweetened Condensed Milk (Eagle Brand)
* 1 cup Nestle's semi-sweet chocolate chips
* 1 cup Nestle's butterscotch chips

Directions

Optional:
- 1 cup coarsely chopped walnuts.
- Spray a 9" square baking pan with cooking spray.
- Press mixture into pan.
- In a preheated oven, bake at 350°F for 30 minutes or until golden brown.
- Cool about 45 minutes and cut into bars.

Barbara Hamane

Barbara Hamane had a nearly 20-year career at the Walt Disney Ink & Paint Department. A premium painter, Barbara was also part of the digital revolution as a Color Stylist with the CAPS production system in the early 1990s. Barbara's shrimp mousse recipe and sour cream chocolate-bit coffee cake were favored offerings at many of the legendary Ink & Paint parties!

Shrimp Mousse

Ingredients

* 1 can cream of mushroom soup
* 1 (8 ounces) cream cheese, room temp
* 1 cup mayonnaise
* 2 envelopes knox gelatin (dissolved in 6 tablespoons warm water)
* 1 cup cooked bay shrimp
* 1 cup celery, finely chopped
* 2 green onions, minced

Directions

In a saucepan, warm soup, add cream cheese and mayo. Blend well. Add dissolved gelatin. Remove from heat. Stir in shrimp, celery, and green onion. Pour into a mold. Chill till firm. Unmold and serve with crackers.

Sour Cream Chocolate-Bit Coffee Cake

Ingredients

* 6 tablespoons soft butter
* 1 cup plus 1 tablespoon sugar
* 2 eggs
* 1 1/3 cup flour
* 1 1/2 teaspoon baking powder
* 1 tablespoon baking soda
* 1 tablespoon cinnamon
* 1 cup sour cream
* 1 (6 ounces) package semisweet chocolate chips

Directions

Mix butter with 1 cup sugar until blended then beat in eggs one at a time. Whisk together flour, baking powder, baking soda, and cinnamon. Mix into butter mixture just till blended then mix in sour cream. Pour batter into greased and floured 9 × 13 baking pan. Scatter chocolate chips over the top then sprinkle remaining 1 tablespoon sugar. Bake at 350°F for 25–35 minutes or until cake just begins to pull away from the sides of the pan. Serve warm or cooled. Cut into squares.

Ink & Paint Artists lounging in their patio. (Courtesy of Valerie Imhof.)

Lois Ryker

Lois Ryker was a talented presence for nearly 30 years within the Painting and Xerox Processing teams at Walt Disney Ink & Paint. Beginning on *101 Dalmatians* (1961), Lois contributed to every Disney animated film through to *The Great Mouse Detective* (1986). Lois' chewy bar cookies were famous within the Ink & Paint corridors and hat's off to former Ink & Paint Department Head Gretchen Albrecht for locating this tasty treat!

Lois Ryker's Chewy Bar Cookies

Ingredients

- 2 tablespoons butter
- 2 eggs
- 1 cup brown sugar
- 5 tablespoons flour
- 1/8 teaspoon baking soda
- 1 teaspoon vanilla
- 1 cup chopped walnuts or pecans
- 1/2 cup coconut (optional)

Directions

Use a 9" × 9" baking pan. Melt butter in baking pan. Beat eggs then add sugar and remaining ingredients including coconut if using. Pour over the melted butter and bake at 350°F for 20–30 minutes. Cool, cut into bars, and roll in powdered sugar.

Ginni Mack

Ginni Mack was a longtime Ink & Paint artist whose career began in 1945 working on the postwar anthology films of Disney Studios. During her early tenure at Disney, Ginni was often called to demonstrate and model for various photo-ops featuring the Walt Disney Ink & Paint process. A petite blonde who often wore her golden strands in a knot-top bun with side-swept bangs, Ginni was asked to model for a tiny pixie. Her various rounds of modeling later resulted in the inspiration for everyone's favorite fairy—Tinker Bell!

Ginni later painted and inked for various animation studios and worked as a Color Stylist for her husband Brice Mack, a longtime Disney background artist and Studio owner. After 20 years of raising her family and freelancing, Ginni returned to Disney Animation where she remained for nearly 20 more years as hand-inking and painting transitioned into digital processes.

Chocolate Angel Cake

Ingredients

* 2 packages (6-ounce each) chocolate chips
* 2 tablespoon sugar
* 3 eggs separated
* 1 pint (2 cups) whipped whipping cream
* 1 Small (8 ounces) angle food cake

Directions

- Melt chocolate chips with sugar over hot water until melted.
- Beat egg yolks until foamy.
- Remove chocolate mixture from heat. Stir in beaten egg yolks and cool for 5 minutes.
- Beat egg whites until stiff.
- Whip cream and add egg whites to it.
- Fold chocolate mixture into whip cream and egg whites.
- Break angel food cake into bite size pieces. Sprinkle the pieces into the bottom of an angel food cake pan, using about half of the cake.

- Cover cake in pan with a layer of the chocolate mixture.
- Cover chocolate mixture with the second half of the cake pieces and finally add the remaining chocolate mixture to form the final layer of the cake.
- Chill in refrigerator overnight.
- Serve chilled. Add fresh berries—if desired. Eat it up, Mmmm Good!!

Ginni's Famous Baked Eggs

Ingredients

- ❊ 18 jumbo eggs—hardboiled
- ❊ 6 cans Aunt Pennies white sauce
- ❊ 2 rows of saltine crackers
- ❊ 1/2 stick margarine (butter)

Directions

- Heat white sauce
- Add milk & margarine (butter) until gravy-like (heavy gravy)
- Smash crackers
- In a greased pan (with margarine), add a layer of crumbled crackers
- Slice eggs and add a layer of sliced eggs on top of crumbled crackers
- Add a layer of white sauce
- Continue to layer—crackers—egg slices—white sauce, to fill pan
- End layers with sauce followed by a topping of crumbled crackers
- Bake to taste. Serves well with ham

Brenda Chapman

Baking by Brenda Chapman. (Courtesy of Brenda Chapman.)

Brenda Chapman is one of the top directors in animation today. At Walt Disney she did story work on *The Little Mermaid* and *Beauty and the Beast* and supervised storyboard on *The Lion King*. At DreamWorks she co-directed *The Prince of Egypt*, and at Pixar she wrote and directed most of *Brave*. She lives in the San Francisco Bay Area with her director husband Kevin (Disney's *Enchanted*) and daughter Emma, the inspiration for Merida in *Brave*.

Banana Bread

(from Brenda Chapman …
who got it from her mom …
who got it from Dorothy Fink in 1967)

Ingredients

* 1 egg
* 1/4 cup butter
* 3/4 cup sugar
* 2/3 cup mashed bananas (extra ripe)[*]
* 3 tablespoons buttermilk[†]
* 2 cups sifted flower[‡]
* 1/2 teaspoon baking powder
* 1/2 teaspoon baking soda
* 1/4 teaspoon salt
* 1/2 cup chopped nuts (optional)

---

[*] Bananas should be brown and soft—the banana flavor will stand out more in the bread. Mash them to a thick soup consistency.

[†] If you don't have buttermilk on hand you can substitute with the following:
  • Add 1 tablespoon vinegar to 1/2 cup milk
  • Let sit for 10 minutes
  • Still only use 3 tablespoons in recipe

[‡] Secret to fluffier bread: sift flower at least 4 times and spoon lightly into measuring cup—do not pat down.

Directions

• Preheat oven to 350°F
• Beat butter, sugar, and egg until blended
• Add smashed bananas and beat to combine
• In a separate bowl, sift flour, salt, baking soda, and baking powder, then add gradually to above mixture along with buttermilk, blending.

Optional:

• Fold in nuts
• Bake in greased 9 × 5 × 3 loaf pan for approximately 1 hour (Push a long wooden toothpick into the center. If it is dry when pulled out, the bread is done. If it has remnants of batter on it, bake a few minutes longer, and continue to test until dry.)
• Remove from pan and let cool right side up
• Makes 1 loaf

Alice Davis

Another recipe from **Alice Davis**, Walt Disney artist, and designer of *It's a Small World*.

Coffee Tapioca

Mix together:

Ingredients

- ✳ 1/4 cup tapioca (minute)
- ✳ 2 1/2 cups cold strong coffee
- ✳ Dash of salt
- ✳ 1/2 cup sugar
- ✳ 1 large teaspoon ground Ghirardelli chocolate

Let stand for 5 minutes.

Directions

- Place in a double boiler and cook over boiling water for 20 minutes or until thick, while stirring often.
- Remove from heat and stir in 1½ tsp vanilla.
- Then spoon into serving dishes and chill.
- Float heavy cream on top of pudding when served and Enjoy!

Coffee Tapioca

Mix together,
    ¼ c tapioca (minute)
    2½ c cold strong coffee
    dash of salt
    ½ c sugar
    1 large t ground (Ghirardelli chocolate)
Let stand for 5 minutes

    place in double boiler
    and cook over boiling
    water for 20 minutes
    or until thick, while
    stirring often.
Remove from heat and stir
    in 1½ t vanilla
Then spoon into serving
dishes and chill.
    Float (heavy cream) on top
of pudding when served
and enjoy!

Coffee Tapioca by Alice Davis. (Courtesy of Alice Davis.)

Bob Clampett

Bob Clampett. (Courtesy of Ruth Clampett.)

Bob Clampett (1913–1984) was a pioneer of American animation. At age 17, Clampett left school to work at the Harmon-Ising Studios where he animated scenes for the first *Merrie Melodies* cartoon ever made, *Lady Play Your Mandolin!*

In 1935, Clampett transitioned to Warner Brothers and was assigned as an animator and key gagman for newly arrived director Tex Avery. It was under Avery's direction at Termite Terrace that Clampett animated the first scenes of Daffy Duck, and developed his trademark sense of zany, irreverent humor. Later on, Avery and Clampett would be part of the team of directors responsible for the creation of Warner Brothers' biggest cartoon star, Bugs Bunny.

Clampett was promoted to Director in 1937, and for the next 9 years he would direct some of the funniest, wildest, and most memorable Warner Brothers cartoons. In 1942, Clampett introduced the beloved canary Tweety (whom he designed after his own nude baby picture) in *Tale of Two Kitties*.

In 1946, Clampett left Warner Brothers. Three short years later, he created a live televised daily puppet show called *Time for Beany* that featured a sea serpent named Cecil and his young, propeller-capped pal Beany. The show would go on to win three Emmys for Best Children's

Program and later be adapted by into the animated cartoon show *Beany and Cecil* which ran for five years straight and was seen worldwide for decades.

Clampett described what he saw as the magic of animation in the following way:

"An artist can take pencil and brush in hand, and on a piece of paper can create a setting, be it an ancient city or a strange planet, and then animate figures doing anything at all that comes to his imagination. No other medium allows the creator to control every detail on every frame so completely."

—Bob Clampett

Bob Clampett's Favorite Chocolate Cake
Baked by his favorite gal, his wife Sody

From Ruth Clampett: My dad had a real sweet tooth. But when you've got three children and all the neighborhood kids hanging out at your house, sweets disappeared fast. So dad was known for hiding away a box of his favorite graham crackers, and it became a great adventure for us to figure out where. Naturally a highlight for us sugar fiends (including dad) was a birthday since mom would bake her famous chocolate cake. Rich and delectable, a piece of this chocolate perfection was enough to satisfy a sweet fiend for days.

Porky's Birthday Party, characters copyright Warner Bros. Ent. (Courtesy of Ruth Clampett.)

Cake Ingredients

* 2 cups flour
* 2 cups sugar
* 1/2 teaspoon salt
* 1 stick butter
* 1/2 cup crisco oil
* 1 cup water

* 3 tablespoons cocoa
* 2 eggs
* 1 teaspoon baking soda
* 1/2 cup buttermilk
* 1 teaspoon vanilla

Directions

Mix flour, baking soda, sugar, and salt in a bowl. Put the butter, oil, water, and cocoa into a saucepan and bring to a boil. Pour into the flour mix and add the buttermilk, vanilla, and eggs and stir up. Pour into a 12" × 18" × 1" pan and bake at 350°F for 25 minutes.

Icing Ingredients

* 1 stick butter
* 3 tablespoons cocoa
* 6 1/2 tablespoons milk
* 1 box powder sugar
* 1 cup walnuts chopped
* 1 teaspoon vanilla

Directions

Melt butter, cocoa, milk, and mix in sugar. Once mixed, spread on hot cake as soon as you take it from the oven. Sprinkle the nuts on top.

Enjoy!

Andreas Deja

Andreas Deja was one of the top artists in the Disney 2D Renaissance. His talents gave life to Roger Rabbit, King Triton in *The Little Mermaid*, Gaston in *Beauty and the Beast*, Scar in *The Lion King*, and Lilo in *Lilo and Stitch*.

Charles Solomon is a well-known historian and author. His credits include *Enchanted Drawings, a History of Animation*, and *The Disney that Never Was*.

From Charles Solomon:

Deja Delights

On a trip to San Francisco several years ago, a friend and I went to a bakery in North Beach and tried *ossi dei morte*, a meringue and almond cookie so crisp and white it supposedly resembles "the bones of the dead." They were good, but I thought the addition of chocolate would improve them—chocolate improves almost anything. After a few experiments, I came up with this recipe. I took some of the first batch to a party at Andreas' and he liked them so well, we dubbed them "Deja Delights." It's not a very sweet cookie, but the cocoa gives it an intense chocolate flavor.

Ingredients

- ❊ 1/2 cup unsweetened cocoa powder, preferably Dutch process
- ❊ 3 large egg whites
- ❊ 1/8 teaspoon cream of tartar
- ❊ 3/4 cup granulated sugar
- ❊ 1/2 teaspoon vanilla extract
- ❊ 3/4 cup toasted hazelnuts

Directions

- Line two cookie sheets with parchment paper or wax paper; preheat oven to 225°F
- Beat the eggs whites at low speed in a large bowl with a mixer, using the whisk attachment. When they're frothy, add the cream of tartar. Increase speed to high and beat until soft peaks form. Add the sugar one tablespoon at a time, beating continuously. About halfway through this process beat in the vanilla. Beat until stiff peaks form and the mixture is glossy. Reduce speed to low and beat in the cocoa, then the nuts.
- Drop by tablespoonfuls onto the prepared cookie sheets. Bake for 90 minutes, then turn off the oven and leave them for about 2 hours. These cookies freeze well.

An informal variation on the normal recipe:

- Add a teaspoonful of instant coffee to the cocoa and substitute unsalted toasted almonds for the hazelnuts.

Susan Goldberg and Eric Goldberg

Susan Goldberg grew up on the west coast of Florida. She is an art director and assistant animator, whose credits include *Pocahontas, Mrs. Doubtfire, Hercules, The Simpsons Movie,* and many others. She won the Annie Award for Production Design on the *Rhapsody in Blue* sequence of *Fantasia 2000*.

Eric Goldberg was born outside Philadelphia. After working in New York and London, he went to Disney, where his animation skills gave life to the Genie in *Aladdin*, Phil in *Hercules*, and Mini-Maui, the tattoo character in *Moana*. He also directed *Pocahontas* and the *Rhapsody in Blue* sequence of *Fantasia 2000*. He is the happy recipient of Susan's cooking.

Baked Cheesecake

Ingredients

Crust:

* 3/4 cup coarsely ground walnuts
* 3/4 cup crushed graham crackers
* 3 tablespoons of melted butter

Filling:

* 4 8-ounce packages of cream cheese
* 4 eggs
* 1 1/4 cups sugar
* 1 tablespoon fresh lemon juice
* 2 teaspoons vanilla

Topping:

* 2 cups sour cream
* 1/4 cup sugar
* 1 tsp vanilla

Directions

- Preheat oven to 350°F
- Rack in center of oven
- 9" or 10" springform pan

Crust:

- Combine nuts, crumbs, and butter and press into bottom of the pan

Filling:

- Beat cream cheese in electric mixer till smooth
- Add eggs, sugar, lemon juice, and vanilla
- Beat thoroughly
- Spoon over crust
- Set pan on baking sheet to catch any butter dripping
- Bake 10" cake 40 to 45 minutes
- Bake 9" cake 50 to 55 minutes
- Cake will rise slightly and may crack in several places
- Remove from oven and let stand at room temperature

Topping:

- Combine sour cream, sugar, and vanilla and put in refrigerator. When the cake is finished baking and has set, spoon topping over top, starting at the center until you are 1/2" from the edges of pan.
- Bake 5 minutes. Allow to cool.
- Refrigerate for at least 24 hours.

Cookie sketch by Eric Goldberg. (Courtesy of Eric Goldberg.)

Here is my aunt's **Sugar Cookie** recipe:

Mrs. Corneil's Sugar Cookie Recipe

Ingredients and Directions

Mix together till smooth:

* 2 eggs
* 2 cups brown sugar
* 1 cup Crisco or lard (my aunt uses lard)

Cream together until smooth:

* 1 teaspoon salt
* 1 teaspoon nutmeg
* 1 cup sweet milk
* 2 teaspoons baking powder
* 1 teaspoon baking soda
* 3 or 4 cups flour (add enough flour to make a fairly stiff dough)

Chill dough:

* Drop balls of dough on cookie sheet
* Bake at 400°F for 8–10 minutes

Sheila Sofian

Sheila Sofian is an independent filmmaker who pioneers in the growing field of Documentary Animation. Her films like *The Truth Has Fallen* (2013) and *Conversations with Haris* (2002) have won awards all around the world. She has taught animation and socially-conscious filmmaking in workshops from Bogota, Columbia, to Yokohama.

Vegan Chocolate Oatmeal Walnut Cookies

Ingredients

- 2 cups quick cooking oats
- 1 2/3 cups all-purpose unbleached flour
- 2/3 cup unsweetened cocoa powder
- 1/2 teaspoon baking soda
- 1/2 teaspoon baking powder
- 3/4 teaspoon salt
- 1 1/2 cups sugar
- 2 tablespoons ground golden flaxseed
- 2/3 cup almond milk
- 2/3 cup coconut oil (if solid heat until liquid)
- 2 teaspoons vanilla extract
- 1 1/2 cups vegan chocolate chips
- 1 cup chopped walnuts

Directions

- Preheat oven to 350°F.
- Mix together oats, flour, cocoa powder, baking soda, baking powder, and salt.
- In a separate bowl combine sugar, flaxseed, and almond milk and mix well.
- Add the coconut oil and vanilla extract into wet mixture and mix well.
- Fold into flour mixture and stir until just combined.
- Fold in the chocolate chips and walnuts.
- Spoon 2-tablespoon scoops of dough on to baking sheet, spacing 2" apart.
- Bake for 11–12 minutes.
- Rest on baking sheet for 10 minutes.
- Transfer to wire rack to cool.

Bibliography

Canemaker, J. (2010). *Two Guys Named Joe*. Disney Editions, Los Angeles.

Illenberger, T. and Avonne K. (1966). *The Cartoonist Cookbook*. Hobbs, Doorman & Company, New York.

Godwin, B. (1996). *Chasens: Where Hollywood Dined*. Angel City Press, Los Angeles.

Johnson, M. (2017). *Ink & Paint: The Women of Walt Disney's Animation*. Disney Editions, Los Angeles.

Kinney, J. (1988). *Walt Disney and Assorted Other Characters*. Harmony Books, New York.

Sito, T. (2006). *Drawing the Line: The Untold Story of the Animation Unions from Bosko to Bart Simpson*. University of Kentucky Press, Lexington.

Scott, R. (1959). *Dolphin Dishes: The Submarine Cookbook*. Norfolk Submarine Cookbook Committee, Norfolk.

Carriker-Smothers, M. (2017). *Eat Like Walt, The Wonderful World of Disney Food*. Disney Editions, Los Angeles.

Periodical

Korkis, J. (2014). *Mouse Planet*, August 20. https://www.mouseplanet.com/10765/The_Tinker_Bell_Cocktail_and_Marc_Davis

Recipe Index

Index by Person or Institution

Walt Disney and his animators eating ice cream, 1936. (Courtesy of the Margaret Herrick Archive, AMPAS.)

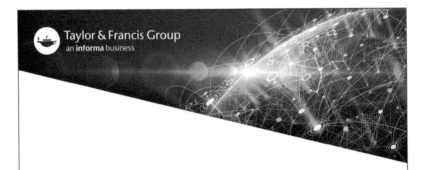